The

Ed Letters

Spinner Publications, Inc.
164 William Street
New Bedford, Massachusetts 02740

Support provided by the Massachusetts Cultural Council.

Cover Illus.: Charles Parsons
Design: Andrea V. Tavares

Library of Congress Cataloging-in-Publication Data

Ashley, Edwin, 1913–
    The Ed letters : memories of a New England boyhood / Edwin and Cliff
Ashley ; edited by Diane deManbey Duebber.
      p. cm.
    ISBN 0-932027-62-8 (pbk.)
    1. Ashely, Edwin, 1913---Correspondence. 2. Ashley, Cliff, 1909---
Correspondence. 3. Brothers--New England--Correspondence. 4. New
England--Biography. I. Ashley, Cliff, 1909- II. Duebber, Diane deManbey,
1948- III. Title.

CT275.A839 A4 2001
974'.092'2--dc21

                                                  2001020656

The Ed Letters

Memories of a New England Boyhood

Edwin and Cliff Ashley

Edited by
Diane deManbey Duebber

Illustrated by
Charles Parsons

Spinner Publications, Inc.

New Bedford, Massachusetts

*To Bob and Lyndsay for their
encouragement and
to Ed with gratitude
and affection.*

Acknowledgments

I would like to acknowledge some generous individuals who helped to make this book possible. Gerry Ashley and Betty Wish supplied photographs and personal memories along with their unique perspectives of life with Cliff and Ed. I am especially indebted to Dr. Charles Parsons, who contributed his artistic talents, which so nicely enhance this volume. I am also sincerely grateful to the people of Marion, who have always been generous in their support of the Council on Aging.

Introduction

Every city or town that has survived any great length of time has a heart that sustains it. Without a heart at the center of its history, it has no foundation for its future. The real history of a place is more than dates and events—it's the pulse of the people who've lived there and interacted with each other and shared common experiences, from the mundane to the sublime.

This book is an x-ray image, so to speak, of the heart of one coastal New England town as seen through the eyes of two brothers who spent their boyhood in Marion, Massachusetts, in the early part of the twentieth century. It is the story of four children and their widowed mother, who worked hard to keep her family together in a time when the world was changing and long-honored traditions were losing their importance. It is the story of a town that nurtured a family and gave it roots. Cliff and Ed Ashley held on to their memories of that time for almost ninety years before I decided to preserve them in this book for future generations.

Cliff was born in 1909 and his brother Edwin in 1913. Their father died while scalloping when Ed was only six months old. They grew up in a house on Clark Street, which at the time was very rural, yet close enough to the village for the boys to befriend most of the merchants and townspeople of all ages and inclinations.

Ed remained in Marion through his adulthood, raising his own family and living out most of his life in the same house on Clark Street. In his later years he became a familiar figure in town, walking the streets routinely, stopping to talk with anyone willing to share a story or two.

He always had time for a story about Marion in the golden days of his youth; in fact, he loved to tell his tales over and over, and we'd all laugh as he described his simple adventures.

Sometimes his stories made him cry, especially when he talked about his sister Grace, who died at the age of sixteen. It seemed that his memory was less selective than some, and we knew that he kept the bittersweet memories as well as the happy ones, although he never lingered on his war years or his own family, preferring to focus on his days as a boy.

Later, when Ed was an old man with failing eyesight and I worked for the Marion Council on Aging, I read his mail to him. It was then that I got to know his brother Cliff.

At the invitation of his employer, Cliff had moved to Falmouth, Maine, as a young man, married, and settled there. But his ties to his brother Ed remained strong, and he was a prolific letter writer, establishing a steady correspondence that would span more than sixty years. Every week there was a new letter from the older Ashley sibling, which I anticipated as much as Ed did. Cliff had his own set of memories of growing up in Marion (along with a wealth of gardening advice and weather commentaries). As I sat in the rocking chair in Ed's apartment reading his brother's accounts of his escapades and the characters he'd known, I realized what a rare treasure these memories were. Why, Cliff even remembered the town's Civil War veterans telling their stories of glory on the battlefield and old whalers boasting of their feats at sea!

After hearing each letter, Ed would carefully bundle it up with the hundreds of others in a special box in his closet. When I left Marion, I thought these letters were too precious to remain in a cardboard box in a closet.

When I approached Ed with the idea of publishing his brother's letters, he was glad to share them. But he had no letters in response; he simply wasn't the letter writer Cliff was, which was just as well because his shaky handwriting was undecipherable. So for this book, I took on Ed's voice in the letters to Cliff, retelling the stories he had told me with all the laughter and tears of one who had never outgrown that period.

With Cliff's permission, I added to his letters to create a bridge between the correspondences and I eliminated references to certain family matters. Also, because people are mentioned who still live in Marion, I left out some names to preserve anonymity. The truth about the people in these accounts can't be verified in every case; the stories here are Cliff and Ed's recollections, not factual research. Recollections tend to lean more toward exaggeration than accuracy, but therein lies their charm.

As the story of the Ashleys began to develop, Charles Parsons volunteered to lend his unique artistic gift to the sketches that enhance this book. I am deeply grateful to him for contributing his talent and encouragement.

Ed and Cliff Ashley are a vanishing asset in a world that tends to view the past as disposable. They have given the town of Marion a gift of enormous value in these letters—one that I hope will not pass away unnoticed, certainly not to those who read this book.

Diane deManbey Duebber
Thompson, Connecticut, 2000

Falmouth, Maine
April 7, 1995

Dear d,

Turned on the outside faucets this morning and painted the sash for my cold frame, but it's too soon to put any seedlings on the porch shelves. I get impatient for spring this time of year.

I remember Cappy Lewis with his dog, Betty, coming to P. C. Blankinship's store in Marion each day to get his paper. Don't know why he got a paper and I doubt if he spent much time reading it. I think he really came to sit on the steps and talk over old times with the gang that used to congregate there. I liked to listen to them and they never minded me. I was just a kid who was fascinated by them and I think they liked that. Most of the old-timers were good to us when we were small.

The Ashley home on Clark Street in Marion

They knew that we had lost our father and they were extra understanding of our pesky ways. But some of these men had been actual whalers and the stories they told could make Moby Dick look like a sardine. Even as young as I was, I soon learned to take these tales with a grain of sea salt, and more whales were harpooned on those steps than ever swam the Atlantic.

I used to ride all over town on my old bike that was too small and too rusty, but it got me where I had to go. I had regular stops like Blankinship's steps, when school didn't get in the way. Remember the fox tails we used to put on our bike handlebars? Old Man Cooper gave us those tails from foxes he had shot at his farm on Point Road, and we were the envy of many a boy with those tails hanging from our handles. I'm sure they made our bikes go faster. We kept them a long time, until they began to look like rat tails, but that was even better. Ma finally made us throw them away. Darn shame. I figure there was many a year left in them yet.

Do you remember Trippy's shanty that was right over the water near Sid Taylor's fish market? I used to hang around there, too. Once, when I was delivering some fish to Dr. Kellogg, he made it clear that Sid was charging too much and called him "that old scup skinner." I thought that was pretty funny. But I don't think the town would like those old shanties there now. Land is too valuable, but when we were kids you couldn't give it away. Funny how times change.

So you spent a dollar on bingo last Tuesday? I may be responsible for some of your bad habits because I had to look out for you when you were small. But gambling, Ed? Gerry says I shouldn't tease you, so go ahead and spend your fortune on bingo.

Love,

Cliff and Gerry

Marion, Mass.
April 15, 1995

Dear liff,

I've been called a scup skinner myself. I wonder what that says about me? Anyway, I hope it's beginning to warm up for you in Falmouth. I know how impatient you get to start digging that garden as soon as the last chocolate Easter egg has been eaten.

Do you remember Bessie Nelson who used to live near Evergreen Cemetery? She was a member of the Cemetery Commission, probably because she wanted to make sure her newly departed neighbors were the proper sort. In those days it was as proper to be buried in the right spot as it was to live in the right neighborhood. I remember one squabble over a cook becoming a resident of the cemetery. Some people objected mightily, but in the end he was granted permission to rest in peace there.

Now, Bessie had twenty-eight cats, give or take a few dozen, and they were like children to her. She couldn't do enough for those cats. I should have remembered this when I found a dead cat on the stone wall near her property. Instead, I tossed the cat into the hole I had been digging for a funeral that morning. A few shovelfuls of dirt covered up the evidence of a trespasser in the grave, and I chuckled as I watched the real burial from a distance. No cat ever had such praying and mourning and preaching over it, and I was very pleased with myself for such cleverness. I finished the job and went home for lunch to tell Nellie what a good and proper and amusing thing I had done. That was probably my second mistake.

Word got around that a cat had been buried in the cemetery with a preacher and all the trappings, and then Bessie got wind of it. She had been missing a cat for a few days and when she heard that I had buried one without her knowledge she was wild with rage. She got the Cemetery Commission to make me dig up the whole plot again, remove the casket, and unearth the very stiff cat who up until then had been enjoying his eternal rest. That was no small job by hand, and she watched every shovelful. But the real clinker was that it turned out not to be her cat after all. She didn't care what I did with the cat then, so after I refilled the grave with its proper tenant, I dug a small private grave for the poor unclaimed cat in a shady corner where no one would bother it. Don't know what all the fuss was about. I wouldn't mind sharing a plot with a cat. In fact, it might be preferable to some of the other residents.

Enough about cemeteries and dead cats. It's time to take a nap. But I do remember those fox tails on our bikes. I don't know why Ma made us give them up just because of a few bugs. Women just don't understand things like that. Too much remembering makes an old scup skinner like me tired.

As always,
Your brother,

Dear d,

It was sixty-one years ago that Gerry and I were married and started our lives together. They have been sixty-one beautiful years. I remember our brother Al always envied our life. One day he said to me, "Gerry made a home for you." And that said a lot in a nutshell. We had hoped that he could spend the winter with us but it was not meant to be. Makes a person very grateful to have another to go through this life with.

We went to dinner out at Cape Elizabeth to celebrate our anniversary. It was nice out there with high waves, but the wind was cold. Took me back to my youth in Marion, and I missed it all over again. I've had a good life here in Maine, but Marion still calls to me, especially when I'm near the coast and I remember the good times we had growing up there. Of course, the most important thing is family, and I have lots of that here in Falmouth, and where there is family, it is home. We had lots of family growing up, too, but you and I are the only ones left.

We were lucky to have such a good family. Times were tough for many folks, but you could always count on family. Makes me think of Mrs. Polly, that nice friend of Ma's. She was one exception. Every once in a while she would show up with a black eye, and she told everyone that she ran into the icebox door. Hannah Nye used to say, "If I ran into the icebox as much as she did I'd take an axe to it!" I thought that was funny back then, but later, when I knew her husband, I got to thinking that Mrs. Nye might have meant she should chop up something other than that icebox.

We sure worked hard as kids, didn't we? I remember working for Mrs. Ryder, who took in boarders, Mrs. Cushing, and

Mrs. Bourne. I earned about twenty-five cents an hour, and that money was like gold to me.

I made the most money in scallop season. Me and Skinny (Reuben Chase) were the first ones in with our limit. Of course, I was always bringing home clams or quahogs, too. I got lots of quahogs around Meadow Island with Charlie Bowman and Artie Charbonneau. Can hardly afford that kind of seafood now, and it isn't as much fun buying it from a market as it was working with friends to bring it in.

Hope spring has come to Marion by now. As I remember, it was a rare occurrence.

Love,

*C*liff and Gerry

Dear liff,

Hope you had a happy anniversary. I lost my Nellie years ago, and I envy the years you and Gerry have had together. Never forget to put her at the top of the list when you count your blessings.

I, too, remember Mrs. Polly and her black eyes. She was a sweet little thing, but I thought she must have been awfully clumsy to keep getting shiners like that. One other friend of Ma's that I liked first rate was Lottie. She was a relative of Mrs. Packard's next door, and she even let us call her Aunt Lottie. Her hair had to be four feet long. It was a pretty light brown with strands of red, and she always teased us about how she got that red in it. Believe it or not, she claimed it was from the red light on Bird Island. She washed her hair in a big glass basin that had once been a lens for the lighthouse out there. She showed it to me once and I was quite impressed.

Aunt Lottie used to make lemon-poppyseed muffins for us kids, and always had just-squeezed homemade lemonade for us too. She was a whiz with lemons. I wonder whatever happened to her or the lighthouse bowl?

Do you recall the family that lived across the street when we were young? I don't remember them much because there were no kids there to interest me, but Bob Taber told me a funny story about running an errand for someone there. A man was working on the roof, and he asked Bob to go to Eddie Blankinship's store to get him a plug of tobacco. Bob walked all the way to the store, which was on Spring Street, only to be told that tobacco couldn't be sold to a minor without permission. So Bob walked back to Clark Street, and the man wrote on a shingle that he had permission to buy the tobacco. Back goes Bob to the store, but now Eddie says he can't buy on credit and must have real money. Once again Bob walked back with a message. By now the roofer was getting hot under the collar, but Bob was getting hot all over. He gave Bob the money and back he trudged, but this time with success. Eddie sold him the tobacco, and Bob walked back for the third and final trip, expecting a big tip for an afternoon's work. He earned one penny that day and has never forgotten it. You know that Bob is a hard worker, but I doubt if he ever had to put so much into earning so little.

I expect he went over to Aunt Lottie's after that for some lemonade. Wish I had some, too.

As always,
Your brother,

d

Falmouth, Maine
May 3, 1995

Dear d,

I wish you could be here to see the flowers in bloom all
around the house and in the borders where the shrubs are. The
rhubarb is up, too, and spreading its huge leaves over the new
grass. I'm really fond of rhubarb. Gerry makes a fine rhubarb
bread with just enough sugar to take out the tartness. I also cut
my first lot of asparagus yesterday. Asparagus is good for two
reasons: it tastes like spring and it makes you feel good to know
that you're not paying those sky-high prices for it at the market.

Now I will have to get the mower out and tinker with it to
get ready for the grass. At least the snowblower will get a rest,
and about time too.

I remember when we were kids how everyone was looking
for the first tautog caught. It was like a contest, and many times
I won. Firpo and I used to run a trawl out on the flat. Many
times we would get a skate and he warned me about the spike
on the tail when I hauled it in. He taught me a lot about fishing
since we didn't have a father to do that for us, and he was awfully
patient. I remember those cold spring mornings out there in
the skiff. I thought heaven couldn't be closer.

Think of me when you go down to Silvershell. We used to
have a lot of fun there when we were kids. Do you remember
the old bath houses that Johnny Mike Allen had down there?
He was always full of stories and never seemed to be without a
paintbrush in his hand, although that didn't stop his chattering.
He was always good to us kids. Everyone liked Johnny Allen. I
hope people will remember me that way some day.

I do remember someone who will never think of YOU
fondly, and that's Rachel Pierce. Remember the trouble you
got into with her pigtail? Seems like you dipped her hair into

your inkwell at school when she was sitting in front of you. But she got the better of you when she shook her head and you got splattered. Caught red-handed. You got a few whacks for that escapade, and Ma was none too pleased to find ink stains on your shirt. What a rascal you were.

Try to stay out of trouble. Inkwells may be out of fashion but temptation never is.

Love,

liff and Gerry

Aunt Lottie's lemon-poppyseed muffins and just-squeezed homemade lemonade.

Dear liff,

Talk about temptation. Even you couldn't have resisted Rachel Pierce's braid if she had been in your class. She had the thickest, longest hair I had ever seen, and sitting behind her every day was just too much to resist. I do remember how mad Ma was, but I don't know how you remember so much about me.

I also remember the bath houses and Johnny Allen at Silvershell, but I don't remember him painting boats. Do you think you got him mixed up with Isaac Newton Hathaway? He spent a lot of time there, too, and I remember him telling us stories of the old-timers. He was what you might call a town character. Used to pay his taxes in pennies. Can you believe that? He'd bring bags full of pennies to the town hall and plop them right down on the assessor's desk. Then he'd give them an extra four cents in case he had counted wrong. That always made him laugh when he told us about that. I guess he was "making a statement," as they say these days.

The spring is here in Marion and turning out real fine. There are some nice flowering fruit trees around Marconi, and the weather is good for walking again. I find my walks take me to the cemetery often, as I've been trying to fix up some flowers on Ma's grave and Nellie's and Grace's, both gone now, and both too young. Our Grace died of Bright's disease when she was only sixteen. Couldn't do anything for her in those days. It changed Ma in a way that even Dad's death didn't. She was still the same Ma and life went on as it does, but it seemed like she had lost some spark that no joy could rekindle. But they're both at rest now, close to each other again, and I like to keep their stones looking good. Planted my Easter lily there and a hydrangea, so I hope they take. It's a long hike for me from Mill

Street, but when I get there it is a nice spot to rest. I can see why Mr. Dodge spent so much time here.

Sometimes I have to search my mind for pictures of them, and other days I forget that they are gone from the earth. I can see Nellie in the kitchen humming over a pot of supper just like I'm there with her. Does that ever happen to you?

What do you mean I didn't do as much fishing as you? I did plenty. Used to go scalloping and sell my catch to Charlie Church for his store. One day I found out that we owed twenty-five dollars, and he said not to worry about it. But that was a considerable sum in those days and I didn't want to be owing, so I spent the whole day scalloping. Only half the work of scalloping is getting them. The other half is cleaning them, and we didn't have a scallop shack so Sunny Moss let me use his. I liked Sunny first rate, but he had a reputation for drinking. Used to hide his whiskey bottles in the shell heaps. I paid back that twenty-five dollars in no time. Charlie Church didn't like Sunny so much. Said he smelled like kerosene, but I think it was the whiskey. Then again, maybe they were the same.

When I need to feel useful, I walk over to the VFW on Route 6 and rake pine needles. Don't know if they notice, but it feels good to be active. Say hello to Gerry from me.

As always,
Your brother,

Falmouth, Maine
June 20, 1995

Dear d,

Clear spring day this morning. I just took a picture of our dogwood tree as it is in full bloom. I wish you could see it. Come to think of it, I wish I could see you. It's been a long time since you've traveled Down East. But I guess our old bones are getting too creaky and cranky to withstand a long car ride. Still, it would be nice.

The old-time roses are doing well, and Dad's favorite will be in bloom soon. Funny how Dad always liked the roses but Ma liked the splashy plants like chrysanthemums. Too bad you never knew Dad. Even I don't remember him much, but once in a while I get a feeling of him. Does that make sense?

The chuck is back. So far he's helped himself to my cukes, beans, cauliflower, and squash plants. I've tried everything except a shotgun, and Gerry says I'm liable to shoot anything with my eyesight, so I let it go. But one of these days I'll get him somehow. The deer don't seem to bother me as much as they do my neighbors. Probably that pesky chuck ran them off so he could have my garden all to himself.

We need rain, but the grass is still growing. Yesterday I put fertilizer on the garden and tilled it in, then I hilled my potatoes for the first time. I still have a lot of weeding to do in the flower beds. If you were here, I would put you to work, just like we did as kids. Funny thing, we worked hard then, but it didn't seem so bad. Guess that is because we expected it and didn't know any other way of life. I think we were better off for that.

Remember how you mowed the lawn of the Music Hall every summer? That was hot work, but you also got ice cream from Petersen's next door, so I think you looked forward to it. I can't understand how they let that grand old building run down. We were always having some dance or play or recital there. I'm glad they're doing something about it now, but I hope the ghost of Mrs. Taber comes back to haunt the irresponsible people who forgot about what a treasure it was.

Maybe she could come on up here and work on scaring off that chuck.

I was just thinking about Ma's name, Louvicy Adda Delano Ashley. Isn't it a pretty name, even for nowadays? Her initials would spell Lada, which is almost like Lady. She was one too.

I feel a nap coming on. Remember to keep your toaster setting on light so you won't burn any more toast and set off the fire alarm.

Love,

*C*liff and Gerry

The old Music Hall

Marion, Mass.
June 29, 1995

Dear liff,

I would like to visit you too, but I don't see how. You had to move so far away that it makes visiting just about impossible. At least we have our letters. I look forward to them, and I have saved them all in a box in my closet. Sometimes if there is no bowling on TV, I like to read them again, and it's like you are here talking to me and telling me what to do all over again. I know you are busy with your gardens and all, but keep writing.

You remembered my first real paying job. I certainly do, too. I mowed the lawn of the Music Hall and got paid twelve dollars for the whole summer. I was proud to be making so much money, but it was hot work with a push mower. I had just about finished on the first day when I heard a whistle from behind me. There was Mr. Petersen from the ice cream shop looking over the fence and motioning me to come over.

"Say, kid" he called "What are you going to do with all those grass clippings?" I hadn't thought about that, and I hadn't planned to rake them up.

"Tell you what. You look like a clever businessman, so I'll make you a deal. I'll trade you all the grass you can rake up this afternoon for all the ice cream I can scoop up into one cone. I could use that grass for mulch and you look like you could use a cone."

Well, I tell you, I didn't have to think twice about that offer. Nothing like Petersen's ice cream after a long hot day of mowing. And that wasn't the only one. Most of the time if he was in the shop we'd make the trade over the fence. I liked him first rate.

Did I tell you that my toaster broke? Now you don't have to worry about my burning toast anymore.

If I got to telling you about all the jobs I have had, I would use up a dozen pens. But I do remember the exact day I left the eighth grade. Maybe I never told you this, but one night I heard you and Ma talking about how tight things were. My bedroom was above the kitchen, and I could hear all sorts of things I probably shouldn't have through the ceiling grate. But I'll never forget that night and hearing Ma crying about not being able to make it through the winter. Boarders were scarce then and taxes were due. Grace was taking in sewing, and Al was already off on his own. Money was so tight it was just about nonexistent.

So the next morning I told Ma that I was quitting school and would get a job. She argued but I won, and I've been working ever since. I don't regret the decision, but sometimes I wonder about other paths. But that's for dreamers, and Ma didn't raise any of them.

The Music Hall is going to be just as grand as ever when they finish. I think Elizabeth Taber would be pleased and will not have to haunt the place anymore.

Have a nice Fourth of July. Marion always has a great parade, and I can walk to the corner of Route 6 to watch it. Maybe there will still be some candy left that some nice kid might throw out for this old codger.

As always,
Your brother,

Ed

Falmouth, Maine
July 5, 1995

Dear d,

We have had enough rain to freshen up the gardens and the squash is really blooming. This is the time of year I miss the spring crops like rhubarb and asparagus. Seems like you just develop a taste for them and it's time to let them rest. That old chuck went through the garden last night and took a bite out of a cucumber, but after that, not much damage. I guess he's getting particular about his pilfering these days.

I have a bad sore throat, so I may have to go see a doctor. Got to support those drug companies, too. Remember how Ma used to always have the ability to conjure up any remedy for the illnesses we could come down with? Whether it was a poultice or a tea, it seemed to do the trick. She used mostly simple things from the garden or the kitchen pantry, but they worked.

I don't think she ever got over not being able to help Grace when she died at sixteen. The doctor said there wasn't anything anyone could do, but I don't think Ma believed that. Ma had always been so strong and kept the family together in sickness and in hard times, and she wasn't one to give up. After Grace, the wind was out of her sails and she was different. When we lost our Judith as a child, I think I finally understood. I can't write about this anymore. Don't know how I got off track in the first place.

Last night's storm was a real gullywumper. Remember the storms when we were kids? Seems like they never ended, just kept rolling back on us when they hit the edge of the water. The best show was around the Marconi towers at the wireless plant. The lightning flashing around them was a sight to behold. Lots of kids tried to climb those towers and some of them succeeded. Didn't you know someone who got stuck up there?

Hope your flower beds are doing well, as I'm sure the weeds are. Funny thing about weeds, they do well no matter what the weather. Stay out of the sun and drink lots of water. At least that's what they tell me. Gerry says don't walk too far on hot days, either.

Love,

*C*liff and Gerry

P.S. When you write on both sides of the paper with a marking pen, it blurs. You should write on only one side of a paper or, better yet, get yourself a real proper pen.

Marion, Mass.
July 11, 1995

Dear liff,

I did like you said and got this good pen. Now I hope you can read my scratchy scrawl. Seems like over the years the lines on the paper have come closer together, so I don't know how much longer I will be able to write to you, unless I find some first-grade paper with fat spaces for old codgers like me.

I do remember the Marconi tower climber, although that wasn't so long ago. He still lives in Marion with teenagers of his own, but when he was a youngster, every boy was dared to climb the last standing tower. Most of them only got close, but he was one who made it.

Of course, there were high fences around the tower which stopped most of the young adventurers, but this fellow managed to get through them and started to climb. His friends, safe at the bottom, urged him on and so up he went, higher and higher. When he could go no further he looked down in triumph, enjoying the cheers of his buddies below. But when it finally occurred to him that what goes up must come down, he froze in fear. He was glued to the top of the tower, and no amount of urging from his friends could budge him. Finally someone ran down Spring Street to the fire department for help, and by the time the siren had finished blasting the town awake, everyone knew that a boy was stuck on top of the Marconi tower at midnight.

The engines came screaming out to the rescue. It was not an easy task given the height of the tower and the size of the boy, but they managed to get him down, much to the relief and embarrassment of his family. I'm sure he lost some of his friends' admiration with a rescue like that, but it made for a good tale to tell for many a year.

You weren't here when the other towers went down, but I remember it like yesterday. The air would whistle with a high pitch and then thunder, as one by one they smacked the ground. Then dust would rise up in big sheets. I was watching from Tabor Academy and could hear it even from there. Seems funny that now I'm living practically in the shadow of the last one in a building named for it.

Rose gave me some licorice the other day, which reminded me of the candy bins in Jigger's (Eddie Blankinship's) store. Those candy bins were an awful temptation to put near a school. Sometimes we'd sneak out of recess to go over there and spend a penny on a string of licorice. Then we'd hightail it back to the playground and stretch it out as long as we could to share it with the rest of the gang. We'd make a rope about as long as the girls' jump rope. Now that was value, and mighty good licorice, too.

Hope you and Gerry are not frying in the Maine sun these days. Save it for winter. You'll need it.

As always,
Your brother,

d

Falmouth, Maine
July 15, 1995

Dear *Ed,*

Another foggy day and about sixty-four degrees. The weather-
men are always promising us a shower, but it never amounts to
much. Ma was a better weather predictor. She could always tell
when a storm was coming by watching the leaves on the trees

A sample of Cliff's letters

turn over to their silver side in the wind. Just about always happened, too, and she didn't need all those fancy scientific instruments to tell her what good, old experience could. My gardens are thirsty, and we are worried about forest fire as everything gets drier.

Gerry is not feeling well, and I try to help all I can, but I think housework is quite a bit harder than garden work. Don't let on to Gerry I said that. On top of everything, I'm getting a bad case of dishpan hands. With Gerry not up to going to church and the heat keeping me home, too, we missed quite a few Sundays. But I went today, and the Reverend teased me about it being "Resurrection Day" when he saw me darken the door of the church. For a young fellow he is pretty good at understanding, and we like his sermons because they are short. I remember Rev. Somers was a good preacher, although not known for being brief in the pulpit, and he was a good man. When men were away during the war, he checked on families regularly, and folks still remember that. A good parson is a good person on the other six days of the week, too.

For some reason the snapdragon in the garden is doing well. Too bad that Gerry's zinnias got cleaned off by the chuck. If chucks were meat eaters instead of vegetarians, I think this world would be in a heap of trouble.

Keep cool and don't take really long walks. Take time to sit in the shade. I'll call on Saturday night if I haven't melted from the heat by then or collapsed from housework.

Love,

*C*liff and Gerry

Dear liff,

Finally got some rain here in Marion, and I hope you got some, too. Is Gerry feeling better yet? She isn't usually one to lay low, but then, this has been unusual heat.

I remember how Ma used to predict a rainstorm when the leaves turned silver. She also said she could hear the frogs croaking extra loud before a rain. Ma sure was smart or else she just had good hearing, or maybe we had frogs that just plain knew more than anyone else. Mr. Dodge used to say that he knew the rain was coming by watching the dandelions in his backyard. They would close up just before a storm. But I think he said that to get out of digging them up like his wife Carrie wanted him to. He said they'd have to stay because they were useful weather predictors, but Carrie would laugh and say they were useful excuses.

Did you ever hear dandelions called Irish daisies? My Nellie used to call them that and I think it was a fitting name for a pretty flower which somehow got misnamed a weed. What I can't figure out is the real difference between a flower and a weed. Is there some list of rules for flowers that weeds miss out on, or is it just that weeds spread like wildfire so they are not so much valued. Seems like there are lots of pretty flowers that are called weeds and just as many mangy-looking ones that are called flowers. You are the gardener in the family, so what do you think? I've mowed over millions of dandelions in my life and I'd just like to know.

I remember Rev. Somers, too, and he was well liked by folks here. But do you remember his son, Henry? Henry was a crackerjack at using a slingshot, and this talent was admired by many of us boys with lesser ability at this art. But one day Henry shot a small stone into the window of a boat, which made a large, shattered hole. Of course, he hadn't planned to break the window, but all of us boys were impressed. Even so, he took off like the devil was after him and I don't think he ever did own up to that misdeed, but I can't blame him. It's hard having a father who is the town's moral yardstick.

We didn't have to live up to anyone's expectations except our own. Ma always let us be what we wanted to be and do what we wanted to do as long as we were considerate of one another. Not a bad way to grow up, and I don't think we turned out so bad.

As always,
Your brother,

d

Dear d,

It is so hot, it is like being stuck in Ma's old, black skillet with the flame up high. Yesterday it was ninety-three degrees and humid, so I was hardly out of the house all day. Years ago, when I was a youngster in my seventies, it wouldn't have mattered so much, but now that I'm in my eighties, Gerry makes me slow down once in a while.

As far as weeds and flowers go, I think the only difference is the stubborn way they grow. Weeds grow no matter what you DON'T do to them, and some flowers won't grow no matter what you DO do to them. When we were boys, we didn't mind the heat. We used to spend a lot of time in the bogs around Marion, but we never harmed anything that was growing or swimming. There used to be lots of snipes on the Sippican Bog and little pickerels in the main ditch. Harry Nye and I put hornpout in the reservoir at Sippican bay. That was fun in those days, but it wouldn't mean much to kids nowadays.

I remember George Nye's old mule. He sure was a big, old boy and had the field all to himself, probably because he was so ornery he wouldn't share. Harry and I were always going to ride him, but we never got up the gumption. Even though he was a mule he was as big as a horse and full of vinegar, especially on hot summer days. He used to kick his back legs up in the air for nothing at all except to show off and warn us kids not to come near him. Funny how daring and exciting that was to us as kids. Today's kids would laugh at us. They do much more exciting things like traveling and watching TV to fill all the idle hours we never knew. Still, the memory of that old mule and all the things we dared but never did with him is fresh on my mind. I guess if I had to pick I'd still choose the excitement of our summer days over what the kids have now. Wouldn't be surprised if that stubborn old mule is still kicking his heels at kids today. He was too ornery to die, anyway.

I remember another story about an iron-willed lady that you told me about years ago, and her name was Miss Austin. Had lots of money and gave some to Tabor Academy for a new racing shell and insisted on naming it "Raybelle." Mr. Wickendon tried his hardest to get her to change it to a more fitting name, but she stood her ground. She gave the money so she could give the name, and I wouldn't be surprised if that old Raybelle is still around today.

Ma certainly worked hard when the summer folks were in Marion. She was glad of the extra house cleaning money, but it didn't seem fair that she worked harder when others were relaxing. One very particular woman on Water Street used to make her clean her piano keys with milk. Can you imagine that? She had to rub the ivory keys each week with milk because it was good for the keys and kept them from getting so brown. Ma used to laugh about that and shake her head about out-of-towners.

Hasn't gotten much cooler since I started this letter. I think the only way to beat the heat is to take a nap. You should too.

Love,

*C*liff and Gerry

Dear liff,

Been hot in Marion too, but seeing as how it is the middle of the summer, I can't complain. Seems like when we were young we worked just as hard in the heat as we did in the cold and never thought to complain about it. Must be we have too much free time on our hands to be bothered by these trifles.

Remember Johnny Bates? No matter what the weather, he was the slowest person I ever did run across. He walked everywhere and was never in a hurry. That must be why he lived so long. One time I was riding with Billy Dodge in his jalopy of a truck, and we came across Johnny pushing a wheelbarrow that looked mighty heavy for such a hot day. Billy offered him a ride, but Johnny just shook his head and kept trudging along.

"No thanks," he said. "I'm in a hurry."

We had a good laugh over that one.

Then there was Neal Potter, who traded in bottles at the corner grocery on Cottage and Spring Streets. He wasn't much to look at but he had a sharp mind. Kept bringing in bottles to Walt Stevens, who owned the grocery at the time. After a while Walt got to thinking that Neal must be drinking like a fish to be returning so many bottles and getting paid for them. Besides, they started to look awfully familiar. So Walt looked out back behind the store where he had been storing them, and discovered that he had been hornswoggled. Neal had been returning the same bottles over and over again and making a good profit. Walt called that thievery, but I called it enterprising.

Sammy Lipmann was another interesting visitor I remember among those who came to buy Ma's produce in the summer. He came from New Bedford with his rabbi to buy chickens from Ma. The rabbi would bless them and mumble some foreign-sounding words over them. And he always wore a long, black coat even in the hottest weather. Big, black hat too. He was very polite to Ma and sometimes brought her tomatoes, but he and the rabbi were always mysterious to me and I felt sorry for how hot they must get wearing those clothes.

Did you know that Ma named me after a famous silent movie star of 1913? I was named after Dad of course, but my middle name, Forest, she said came from a star that all the young women swooned over. Good thing his name wasn't Elvis.

As always,
Your brother,

Dear d,

Rainy here this morning, and they say it may keep up for a couple of days. With the fire hazard as high as it is, I can't complain about it.

My garden is coming back after sowing it a second time, but I did see a chuck and a rabbit in the back lot. They'd better not help themselves to my garden this time or I'll make rabbit-chuck stew out of them. Come to think of it, that would probably be a tasty combination.

My rose bushes have been doing well despite the dryness. Maybe that's because of the coffee grounds I mulch them with. Dad's favorite, the American Pillar, is still in bloom, although it is beginning to fade a little. Funny how memory picks out little things like that to store away. Dad's been gone almost seventy-five years now, but I still remember how he liked those roses. I was looking at my old class picture and trying to remember names for the faces. I know nine of them have died and most of the others have moved on to other places like I did. Not too many of your generation still left in Marion who have been there all their lives.

I was thinking about all the activity on Hiller Street when we were kids. It was a good place just to hang around, and we knew all the workmen there. Do you remember the pig episode at the blacksmith shop on Hiller Street where they make sails now? Rufus Briggs was bringing a load of pigs to the market in Mattapoisett when a thunderstorm hit. He pulled into the blacksmith shop, but the wagon was too long to fit all the way. He and the horse were dry and relaxed, but when the storm was over, he found that the downpour had filled his wagon and all the pigs had drowned.

Do you remember when they brought coal into Long Wharf and Hiller had the two wheeled carts to haul it up to the coal pocket? I remember that Herb Gurney was one of the crew on the schooner that brought the coal in to the wharf. I always enjoyed watching them land and unload. Coal was awfully important in those days. Not so much now. Things change like that and so do we. But don't you remember feeling important as a kid? That doesn't change. Maybe it was Ma who helped us to feel that way, but I think a lot of it was just knowing our place and feeling secure in our own town. The folks in Marion were like a big family to us. We were very lucky as kids, Ed. It's something to think about and never forget.

Love,

*C*liff and Gerry

Dear liff,

Why don't you mix up a batch of chuckrabbit stew and send it down here? Sounds good. I might even like it better than JELL-O.

I do remember about the pigs. What a surprise it was to Rufus Briggs to find they had all drowned while he and the horse were waiting out the storm. We've had some real gullywumpers here, and we saw plenty as kids.

Our rent has gone up now and we have to pay extra if we have an air conditioner. Seems like I never get the hang of prices these days. I figure that the cost of running the air conditioner for a summer is equal to the cost of three weeks board at the old Sippican Hotel.

I still remember that place. What a grand, old hotel it was in its heyday, but, when we knew it, a lot of its old glamour had worn off. But it was still a fine place to pass the summer, and it only cost thirteen dollars a week to stay there—meals included. The folks sitting on the porch rocking away their days looked so fine, and I used to think how lucky they were to be able to have such a summer of leisure with no hay to bring in or laundry to deliver.

Another summer visitor of much importance was FDR. Were you with us when we went to watch for him at the corner of Hiller and Main? Come to think of it, we weren't kids by then, so you must have been in Maine. There was always a bunch of us hanging around as if we had nothing better to do, and we were grown men. Once in a while I did see him in his wheelchair with Dr. MacDonald. I liked Dr. MacDonald. He always had time to be nice to folks. Only thing is he didn't see eye to eye with FDR when it came to politics, and he had many a lively conversation with him about that. One time he said to me: "I may have helped his legs, but I couldn't fix his head!"

Summer in Marion was full of new faces, but we always knew our own. Now I have time to sit and rock like those guests at the Sippican Hotel, but it's not the same. So much is gone— the hotel, FDR, and the summers of our childhood. But I still have the memories. God willing, I'll always have the memories, and you will too.

Don't think I'll pay for the air conditioning. I'll just sit outside in the shade.

As always,
Your brother,

Ed

Dear ,

I had to do something to end this dry spell, so yesterday I washed my car. Sure enough, it rained this morning. Hardly ever fails. This has been one of the worst growing seasons I can remember. When the blueberries were flowering, it was dark and rainy, and the bees were too wet to work. So instead of the usual forty quarts, I ended up with about six. I was very disappointed. And Gerry makes great blueberry pie.

The grape vines are loaded, though, and I expect a good harvest—not that grapes are as much anticipated as blueberries. I know it is about time for the coons to move in and check them out. They follow a calculated calendar and hardly ever forget to visit us. Gerry saw a pair of skunks out under the pear tree last night, but so far they have not bothered us. They do like to dig up the grass looking for beetle grubs. Wish they'd work on scaring off the coons.

I remember one time when I was up to the Farmers Exchange, as they called it when Spooner ran it. We just called it the old depot. Monk Hale and Fred Cathcart had locked arms and were jigging it out on the front porch. That was a sight to see and we enjoyed it very much. Needless to say, they were well oiled with moonshine. Boy, some of the old crew were hard to beat.

And then there was Mrs. Barden, who came in to play the piano for the silent movies. She was good and made exciting music, so we always gave her a big hand. All the kids used to try to get to the movies on Saturday afternoons up in the Cozy Theater, and it only cost a dime. The movies were run in serials and would end just at the exciting part, so we for sure would have to come back the next Saturday. We couldn't wait, and I especially liked the cowboy movies. Wouldn't waste seven dollars on movies nowadays, and besides, they hardly make cowboy movies any more. I'd rather watch the old shows and hear Mrs. Barden banging away at the piano again.

So you were able to get five tomatoes from your plant. I hope that won't upset the market in Marion. Enjoy your summer.

Love,

*C*liff and Gerry

Marion, Mass.
August 20, 1995

Dear liff,

I remember Mrs. Barden, too. The way she played that piano was hair-raising! I wonder if she cleaned those piano keys with milk like Ma said the rich summer people did. But mostly I remember the movies. Tom Mix was my favorite cowboy, but I always wondered why he wore lipstick. Didn't seem right for a cowboy, but that was Hollywood. Of course, the movies were in black and white, but even so. Cloggy Whistle Trigger agreed that it had to be real lipstick.

Then there was Romey Davis, Dr. Kellogg's black cook. He was as much a wonder as Mrs. Barden. Not because of his cooking, which was almost as good as Ma's, but because of the things he dared to do. One day a tramp came to the door to ask for some food. Romey dished him up a nice plate of dinner, but he happened to catch him throwing it all away. The tramp was muttering something like he wasn't going to take food from a black man, only it wasn't as nicely put as that. And Romey heard him. It was like slapping a whale with a sardine. He grabbed a meat cleaver and chased that old tramp halfway to Mattapoisett. Romey told me he came so close to catching him that he chopped the tramp's coattails into checkerboards. I didn't know if I was supposed to laugh or not.

Romey was well known for his temper, but I always liked him first rate. Once we were in a boat together fishing and somehow he fell in. He couldn't swim, but if you remember, there was quite a lot of him and he thrashed around like a hurricane yelling, "For God's sake, get me out of here, I'm freezing and I'll never eat another fish again!" Don't know what all the fuss was about. It was only September. Anyway, I hauled him out, but he never came with me in the boat again. After that, we fished from Old Landing and caught tinker fish. He must have forgotten his vow to give up eating fish.

We were friends, Romey and I, and he was always kind to a pesky kid like me. I never thought of him as a black man. He was just Romey. When he got older, he went blind and one day he said to me, "Ed, everything is black to me now." Romey retired from Dr. Kellogg's and returned to the south, but I still remember him clear as day, and it always makes me smile.

Too bad your blueberries were a flop. Maybe you'll have to learn to make Billy Dodge's dried apple pie instead. Ask Gerry if she has a recipe for that. Sure would be good to match the old tastes with the old memories again.

As always,
Your brother,

Falmouth, Maine
August 24, 1995

Dear d,

Another foggy day. Do you know I have tried three pens before I found one that worked? What is this world coming to?

We have had more than our share of fog this summer and I feel sorry for the fellows who are trying to get their hay in. Brings to mind the old story of the fog being so thick you could lay shingles on it.

The garden is doing well and we are picking a few more blueberries now, although they seem more sparse than in years past. I expect a big crop of raspberries in the fall as they are ever bearers. I have cukes, summer squash, lettuce and beet greens, and sunflowers for our hungry winter birds. We'll have potatoes, squash, and onions enough to carry us through the winter.

Do you remember how Ma used to can practically everything that grew, and made all kinds of jams and jellies for the racks in the cellar? By fall those racks were so heavy it looked like the wall was made of glass. But as the cold Marion winter pressed on, those stacks dwindled and the cellar seemed to get darker. The glassy glow seemed to disappear, and by the spring it was just a dark cellar again. Ma made the best grape jelly and brandied peaches I ever had. What a treasure it was to go down cellar and pick out a new jar after Ma had just baked Saturday bread. I don't know which was better, the smell or the taste.

I think this pen is about to run out, too. I know I've said this before, but today I have a real sense of blessing to have my children and grandchildren near. They are all taller than I am and they pat me on the head calling me Shorty. Makes me chuckle. They're good kids and I'm real proud of them. But I can't deny the signs of old age. I sometimes have to stretch out and take a nap in the afternoon, something I thought I'd never admit to. I used to think it was only for old folks, but Gerry tells me I'm approaching that station in life already since I am eighty-six. What happened to the boys we used to be not so long ago in Marion? I think they're still inside somewhere but they have to live with these old bodies we've taken on. Kind of like the glass disappearing from the cellar shelves.

Now my pen has really quit, so I must too. Might even take a nap.

Love,

*C*liff and Gerry

Dear liff,

I know what you mean by the glassy wall in the cellar. It was a good feeling to go down there in the fall and see all that food stacked up, looking so promising and shiny in the glass jars. Ma never let me in the kitchen when she was boiling those jars, but I often got to lick the pans. I never could figure out why it was called canning when there were no cans involved. I always thought the word should be jarring, but later I found out that jarring had already been taken. Anyway, it was nice to see so much food for a family that lived from day to day on whatever money we could all scrape together. I think that was more important to me than anything else.

Do you remember John Sabin, who worked for Edith Austin on Water Street? I was thinking about him today when I saw Canada geese all over the lawn of the VFW. He loved the geese and used to put out bread and lettuce for them. This brought huge flocks to the estate, but I guess it didn't bother Miss Austin like it would some folks. She never told him to stop feeding them, so they just kept coming. Many of the geese stayed all year, and I wouldn't doubt if some of their descendants are still coming back.

Miss Austin must have thought highly of John Sabin because she had a house built for him on Cottage Street. He lived there for many years with his daughter, Vera. Do you know that Vera still haunts that house according to several families that have lived there since? I know the family that lives there now, and they have tried to pick my brain for more information about her, but I can't seem to recall much more than the geese. Seems that they've had glimpses of Vera in the upper bedroom, where the door slams and lights turn themselves on.

She likes balloons, too. One day a balloon floated from the dining room, up the stairs, around a corner, down the hallway, and then into the hands of the lady of the house. She is sure Vera delivered it to her because a balloon could never float in such a pattern. Several times the hem of Vera's skirt was seen as she rounded a corner, often going toward the attic. The family who lived there in the '60s actually saw Vera in person in a corner of the attic. Don't know if I put much belief in all this, but it's fun to speculate.

I imagine Marion has had its share of ghosts in any number of houses. I even heard of one in the Music Hall. When it's my turn to knock on the pearly gates I don't think I'll sign up for a term of haunting. I still have my memories clear and intact, and I think I'll just take them with me. Besides, it will be good to see Ma, Al, Grace and Nellie again, and get to meet Dad. I'll be busy enough.

As always,
Your brother,

d

Dear d,

This has been a funny day. No sun and very damp, and it's raining now on Sunday morning. Gerry and I didn't go to church this morning, but don't think we are sinners for skipping it. The church closes up for August, but I expect God doesn't.

Today I was thinking about school in Marion. I think it was around eighth grade that we went to the Manual Training School on the other side of the A&P where the Masons are now. At one time Teddy Pierce had his plumbing store there, and Al worked for him.

Sometimes I get to thinking about Al, and I wonder what he would have been like if he had lived to be an old codger like us. He didn't have an easy life, but I envy the way he died. While most people leave this life kicking and screaming, he just went to bed one night and didn't wake up the next morning. The woman who ran the boarding house said she found him looking as if he were peacefully asleep the next morning.

I must be getting senile to start talking about school and end up with Al.

I have tendonitis in my left arm and shoulder and it bothers me a lot. Good thing it's not in my writing or weeding arm.

These days, if you do any gardening, you are at the mercy of the weather. I expect even Eden was dependent on too little or too much rain. But we do know the soil was right for apples. I wonder if Adam put cut hair on his beans. It works for me but I don't know if that's because it's good fertilizer or because it keeps the coons away. And tea leaves are supposed to be good for roses, or at least that's what I've been told. But we don't drink enough tea to make it worthwhile to put the leaves out. But it all comes down to rain.

We used to have to dodge the rain when we were trying to get Grandpa's hay in. Wouldn't Grandpa wonder at the rigs they have today? I like to see the rolled bales of hay. They look pretty in the fields and I know they are not so much work as those square bales were. Grandpa was real careful not to waste a fork full of hay. I still remember how hot the mow was when I rolled the hay back and tramped it down. The only thing hotter was me, and itchy, too.

Nothing like heading down to Silvershell after a day of haying in August. The salt water scrubbed all the dust and itches off my skin, and took the tiredness out, too. I wonder if it's as much fun these days with all the riding contraptions there are. Hardly seems like work but it must be less itchy. Either way, a swim at Silvershell makes it all worthwhile.

I see they are changing the traffic lights at Route 6 and putting in crosswalks. Don't forget to push those little white buttons and take your white cane. Gerry says that God is on vacation along with everyone else, so say a prayer for us in church.

Love,

*C*liff and Gerry

Dear liff,

What do you mean your church is closed? If you think it is too hot for folks to sit through a service, think about how hot it is in the OTHER place. Seems to me that it would be a good reminder.

I remember how hot it was in the summer at the old Universalist Church before it became the Marion Art Center. Seems like the preacher didn't care, but those cardboard fans were going like windmills. Remember I had a job there? It wasn't a hard job, and, truthfully, I rather liked it because it was quiet and cool and I was alone.

I was the organ pumper, working the air pump in the basement. It was my job to pump for the hymns for the organ in the loft, and I tell you it was a good muscle builder for the arms. But in between the hymns I could do what I wanted as long as I was ready when the organist wanted me.

One summer day it was awfully hot down there, no dampness to cool it off. So I wasn't feeling too active and was just lying around when, what do you know if I didn't fall asleep. Suddenly there was a loud thunder sound in my dream, and I sat right up like the dead. Seems like the whole congregation was waiting to sing, and the organist was rattling the air pipe to let me know that I was holding up the service. Lordy, did I pump fast. Don't know why I didn't get fired from that job, but I guess no one else wanted it. Makes me laugh to think of it now.

The summer seems to be stuck in place with little break in the weather. It must be hard for the farmers, always wondering, watching, and praying that all their hard work won't be wiped out in an afternoon. I also remember working the hay at Grandpa's farm over by Gifford's Corner, and how hot we got. We used to walk down Clark Street and cross Converse and go through the woods. We often stopped at Aaron's Run to splash in the stream a little first. After a long day of working on Grandpa's hay mow, it was a good spot to accidently fall into before we got to Silvershell where the real fun began.

Betty Wish said to say hello to you when I next wrote, so I guess this is it. She is doing well and says she can feel the spirits of her ancestors all the way back to the Blankinships around her in a peaceful way in the house. Betty's family has always been good neighbors. Her mother, Mrs. Packard, was kind to us. One day she hired Bob Taber and me to cut down a cherry tree in her back field, just like George Washington, except that we had permission. Seemed like a shame because it was a nice tree. But we did it, and Bob decided to mark the tree trunk so that it wouldn't be forgotten. He carved into it: "This tree was felled by axe in 1926." I wouldn't doubt that you could still find it today, although what were once fields on her farm are now overgrown with forsythia and bittersweet. I'd like to find that trunk again. No particular reason except that it would bring back those days and make them seem real again. That would be nice.

Hope you are keeping cool. If not, go find a stream to jump into. Wouldn't that be a sight! Also, give my regards to Gerry.

As always,
Your brother,

Falmouth, Maine
September 22, 1995

Dear d,

I just got back from the cemetery. I went out there to plant some bulbs around the stone on our lot. We lost our little Judith decades ago, but she is never far away in our thoughts. I like to think of her as being with Ma. They would have liked each other. The bulbs always look nice in the spring. Guess there are no chucks out there to get at them.

Today would be Ma's birthday. Do you remember how she loved the chrysanthemums that grew near the front porch?

Ed Ashley

She and Gram had a lot of influence on me when I was a youngster because they were interested in all kinds of plants.

I am eighty-six and this has been one of the worst growing years that I can remember.

Do you remember Mr. Dodge who painted our house once with a five-gallon bucket that never ran dry? He lived on the corner of Pleasant and Pitcher Streets in a rambling house with a wonderful rock in the front. Didn't we have fun on that rock? Can't quite recall, but he never did get over his wife's passing. Nice man though.

The trees are starting to turn, and soon we will have all shades of earthy colors. This strange summer is over, and I only hope the fall will be better. Mostly I hope we don't get an early frost because there is still growing left to do in my garden before I put it to bed.

I sure am glad you are in that place and that they are looking out for you. It's a shame that we are so far apart.

You once said that you got your bad habits from me when I had charge of you when you were a baby. What bad habits? All I know is you sure were an ornery baby.

Love,

*C*liff and Gerry

Marion, Mass.
September 29, 1995

Dear liff,

The trees in Marion are starting to turn, too. Hope we don't have a gale that will strip them before their time. Seems a shame to wait so long for autumn and sometimes it's gone overnight because of the wind.

What do you mean I was an ornery baby?

I do remember old Mr. Billy Dodge and his peculiar ways. What a fine house he had and he never minded us kids racing up and down his rock. We had great times on that rock. Everyone said an Indian was buried under that rock but no one could prove it, and I think they were mixing it up with the rock in the Tabor Academy woods. Now if ever an Indian was going to

Billy Dodge chained his folding chair
to a tree near Carrie's grave.

be buried under a rock, he would for sure pick that one. Split right down the middle, too. Only the brave ones dared to walk through it. Only the thin ones, too. But Billy Dodge's rock was perfect for all of us kids.

Do you remember his dried apple pies? I do. He used to peel apples in the fall, slice them real thin, and then thread them onto long strings. Then he'd hang them in the windows to dry. And it wasn't Mrs. Dodge who made the pies but Billy himself, and if we happened to come by on the right day, he would give us a piece. My, that was good pie. More chewy than Ma's but real tasty.

I remember he told us about Miss Elizabeth Taber, who paid him to plant the elm trees along the Marion roads. He made a dollar a day and was glad of it, and he was very proud of those trees. She kept a careful eye on his work to make sure he was spacing them properly, and he did exactly as she wanted because she didn't give out wages like that freely.

Yes, he did paint our house. I remember that now. One day he knocked on the door and told Ma that he happened to have a five-gallon bucket of paint left over from his house painting and wondered if she would be interested in having him use it on our house. Painting a house was a luxury in those days, at least for us it was. It was all a poor widow could do to put food on the table. So she gladly accepted and paid him with a meal now and then. He worked in the late afternoons when he had time and that bucket was bottomless. It never seemed to be empty, and before we knew it the whole house had been painted.

Billy Dodge and his wife Carrie always took an evening stroll down Pleasant Street, walking hand in hand and chatting comfortably. Sometimes they'd stop to talk with Ma. But when Carrie died, he got strange. Every day he would walk by our house on Clark Street on his way to visit her grave in Evergreen Cemetery. But the odd thing was that he talked with her, and I don't mean under his breath. He really did carry on conversations with her as if she were standing there with him. I heard him once when I secretly followed him. One of those bad habits you know nothing about.

Got so as Billy Dodge was spending so much time at Carrie's grave that he brought a folding chair with him and chained it to a nearby tree. He did this for twenty-four years, no matter what the weather. That chain grew into the tree and outlasted several folding chairs. Even today you can see a lump around the girth of that tree where the pine grew right over it. Theirs was a love that neither time nor death could destroy. We all thought he was crazy, but in time I came to admire him, and I never forgot his kindness to our family.

Next time you're at the cemetery, say hello to Judith from her uncle Ed who still lives in Marion.

As always,
Your brother,

Indian Rock in Tabor Academy woods where
Indian Chiefs are said to be buried

Dear d,

We got some rain last night, and now everything is a soggy mess, but it ought to give the garden a boost. At least it will help the grapes if the coon doesn't get them all. That coon's not as pesky as the chucks, but he does like grapes. I may have to get in the squash, as they expect it to turn cold again soon. I have carrots and beets in the ground, and the parsnips won't be dug until next spring.

At this time of year I always think of the way it was when the scallop season started. Remember all the shanties on the wharf? A lot of fellows took their vacations at that time to go dragging for scallops. The buyers would be at the docks to weigh them out and pay cash on the barrel head for your day's work. Now that was exciting. We'd think about it all summer and plan how we would use the pay. Just going out with my skiff I could make up to fifteen dollars a day, and that wasn't bad for those times. Of course, I gave a lot of it to Ma to help run the house, and that made me feel good.

When Grandma paid me for painting her porch, I used to give it to Ma too. I felt like the man of the house to be able to help her with expenses and, let me tell you, it was hard work. Grandma was very particular about sloppy work and had a fondness for tradition, like when it came to painting the porch, the ceiling had to be light blue. Always the same blue. One time I started to paint it white because I was out of that blue, and you would think I had committed the worst sin. She practically threw me off the porch and told me not to come back again until I had found the proper blue.

"All New England porch ceilings are painted blue," she sputtered, "so that the wasps can't make nests in the corners.

Bees don't like the color blue and that's a fact. Besides, it's traditional, just like red barns." I knew better than to question her logic, so I put off finishing the job until I had just the right paint. And to this day I have never found a wasp nest under a blue porch roof.

I'm glad you look out for the ladies at Marconi Village. Ma would have liked that, and Grace too. Carrying groceries and dumping the trash is a nice touch. Keep it up.

Love,

Cliff and Gerry

Scallop shanties on the wharf

Dear liff,

Awfully rainy here, too, but at least I don't have to worry about a soggy garden. I remember Grandma's blue porch ceiling, and lots of Marion houses still have the color of the sky under their roofs, but I doubt if it has any practical purpose. Does look nice though.

I also remember how good it felt to turn over money to Ma, although Grandma never hired me to paint. I wonder why? Ma was always good to the people she hired and never skinflinted anyone. One time when the sidewalk out to the street needed repair, Ben Pina came over and asked her if he could do it. Ma knew the job needed doing and that Mr. Pina needed the work, but she hadn't budgeted for it at that time. But Mr. Pina gave a quote that she couldn't turn down so she hired him. It took him quite a while, and I remember him sharing lunch with us or a lemonade to break up the long, hot hours he put into that sidewalk. Somehow Ma came up with the money and that sidewalk still looks good today.

Years later, old Ben said to me, "You know, Ed, your mother was the only white person who ever invited me into her house, and I never forgot that. She was a first-class lady." I like to remember that, and he was right.

But not all workers felt so good about their jobs. Did I tell you about the writing found in the Congregational Church basement ceiling? Seems like they took down the ceiling to do some repairs and found an interesting statement written on a beam by a carpenter forty years ago. It said in big black letters: "By the time you read this I will be in Hell." And it was signed, too. I remember him, and his family still lives in town. They decided to cover it over again with a new ceiling so it wouldn't shock anyone else for another generation. Don't know why he felt that way, but perhaps no one ever invited him into their house for lemonade. Makes a person stop to think about the little things that are more important than we know.

Keep out of the rain, and I hope those chucks are giving you a rest.

As always,
Your brother,

Falmouth, Maine
October 26, 1995

Dear d,

Cloudy and chilly this morning. Looks like it's going to be a cold Halloween. Better give the trick-or-treaters hot chocolate instead of candy this year. Wonder if they'd like squash.

The leaves are coming down fast now, but not as colorful as some years. The maple on the front lawn just turned brown and had no color at all. If I'm going to go to all the trouble of raking them up, I'd like to at least enjoy the color first.

Your writing is getting better. Keep it up, and don't lose the new pen. It doesn't smudge like the marker you were using before.

We used to get cranberries off the bogs at this time of year. Just gathering around the edges was enough. Ma made the best cranberry pudding with lots of sugar to take out the tartness. Cranberries are showing up in everything nowadays, even meatloaf.

As I get older and look back on our life, I wonder how Ma kept the family together through those early years after Dad died. I remember that day clearly, although you wouldn't. You were only about six months old. He was just going scalloping and would be back for supper. But he had a heart attack and fell out of the boat. Good thing he wasn't alone or we might never have found him. He was only forty-four. You would have liked him. I did. Over the years I have tried to live up to what Ma taught us as we were growing up. Good sense and kindness were big on her list. I am lucky to have my children and grand-children around me, and I sure am proud of them. I think Ma would have been too. I have had a good life.

Do you remember Uncle Reuben hauling off shells and dumping them on the back lot? In another century some kids will be exploring back there and will think they have found an old Indian heap. Remember the big shell heap by the old yacht club near Silvershell? That's where we found lots of arrowheads, and Ernie Clark found the most, along with Henry Taber. I wonder what ever happened to Ernie's collection? He pretty much cleaned out all the arrowheads in Marion. We used to find them everywhere, in stone walls and fields alike.

Glad you got dishes for the microwave. We'll make a cook out of you yet. Why don't you try making some cranberry pudding?

Gerry and I send our love,

liff

Marion, Mass.
October 30, 1995

Dear *C*liff,

If you really want my opinion, I don't think kids will like to get squash for Halloween. But I'm sure your friend the chuck would like some.

I think you were right in saying that Ernie cleaned out all the arrowheads in Marion when we were kids. Wish I still had some, but they've disappeared in the dust of time like my nail ring from John Swift.

Seems like my memory of those early days is more sharp than my thinking nowadays, and those items were lost in the nowadays. You know that old saying, "Of all the things I've lost, I miss my mind the most?" Sometimes that's me. I was trying to think of my earliest recollection and it came to me that it was the washtub moon.

Remember how Ma used to do cleaning to earn money for our family? She took in laundry and cleaned houses. A hard worker she was. Well, one night she took me with her to the Masonic Hall building on the corner of Spring Street and Cottage Street, where she was washing the big floor on the second story. Don't know where you were, or Al, or why she took me, but it was just Ma and me. It was one of those clear October nights around 1916 that was full of the smell of yellow leaves and wood smoke.

We climbed up what seemed like a hundred stairs to the top of that skyscraper, and while Ma cleaned I could run around in that vast space to my heart's content. It was the tallest, widest space I had ever known. Then my eye caught sight of an old wooden ladder leaning on a wall, and of course I had to climb it. Without her seeing me, I made it up to the top where a small window looked out on the world below and above, and I was astonished. I called out, "Ma, come over here quick. The moon is as big as your washtub and I think I can reach it!"

I was convinced that if I climbed out the window I could touch the moon. To this day I remember my wonder. Our poor mother screamed and just about flew up that ladder to rescue me. But I didn't need rescuing. She brought me down with a pounding heart that I could feel through her sweater. She made me stay by her side all night while she cleaned. Just couldn't understand what I had been trying to tell her—that the moon was as big as the roundest washtub I had ever seen and was within reach. The world was new to me then, a place of all possibilities, and I wanted to touch the moon.

Of course, I outgrew that feeling as I gained the "wisdom" of age, but lately I have come to think that I may have hit upon some truth there. We can reach for the moon. No guarantee that we'll touch it, but it's the reaching that counts.

Don't know what ever happened to Ernie's arrowhead collection. I was too busy trying to touch the washtub moon. Be well, and Gerry too.

As always,
Your brother,

Falmouth, Maine
November 5, 1995

Dear d,

This fall has not been outstanding, but it has been a lovely day today. Not too cold, and lots of sun. Fall in Marion used to be my favorite season. Maybe the blueness of the water made the colors of the leaves brighter, but I remember the beauty and peace of that time of year more than any other.

You said you went to the Methodist Church, but when we called Betty Wish she said you were at the Congregational Church. Are you such a sinner that you have to go to two churches?

I cleared off most of the gardens, but I am still harvesting some things. I have a row of parsnips that I will dig sometime next spring. I'll leave a few things for the deer and the chucks, but come summer they'd better watch out. Fair is fair. I still have to rake more pine needles over the flower borders.

Remember how I used to sell my statice to Mrs. Dexter? She was one of my first customers who appreciated my knack with flowers. Encouragement like that helped me to pursue my life's work with gardens.

Ma used to get groceries from W.C. Dexter in Mattapoisett, and Clarence Ransome would deliver the orders. We had several little grocery places in Marion, but we also had lots of fruit and vegetable delivery wagons that went from house to house. Wasn't it fun when they came? I also remember the rag man coming.

How are you coming along with your new microwave? I hope you don't have to have the fire department come calling on you early in the morning like so many times before. Don't know why you can't eat cereal for breakfast like everyone else. I guess Ma spoiled us as kids. She always put up a good breakfast with lots of eggs. Back then it didn't matter how many eggs we ate, and I have a suspicion it doesn't now, but we do as we are told by mothers or wives, and life goes on.

Gerry has finally gone back to using the dryer instead of hanging the laundry outside. We like to save on electricity during the summer, and, besides, clothes always smell so nice when they have spent the day outside. At least she doesn't make me soak the clothespins like Ma did. Do you remember how she used to make us lug a bucket of clothespins down to Silvershell and soak them in salt water so that in the winter they wouldn't freeze to the clothesline? Must have worked because we had to do it every year. But it wasn't so bad. We used the day for fishing or quahogging. Still, I didn't like running into any of the other boys because they would tease me about women's chores. I bet they soaked their mother's clothespins in secret too. Don't tell Gerry about this or she'll send me off to the coast with a bucket of new wooden clothespins.

Take care and enjoy this fine season. Keep going to all those churches.

Love,

*C*liff and Gerry

Marion, Mass.
November 11, 1995

Dear liff,

It's warm in Marion too, and it has been a nice fall. The leaves have stuck to the trees longer than usual. I like fall too, and my walks get more rambling, but I have to watch out for early darkness.

I DID go to two churches, but one was not for praying. I'm not such an old leatherman that I don't know where I'm going and why. I went to the Methodist Church for a chicken pie supper and the Congregational Church for Sunday morning. Don't think I'm such a sinner that I need both, but then again it can't hurt. Besides, those Methodists are real good cooks and put on a fine supper.

Remembering the grocery wagons and produce carts takes me back a mighty long way. One of my favorites was Mr. Whitmarsh who came around selling yard goods in his old wagon pulled by Gracie, a bony horse that was somewhat skittery. Ma spent the longest time looking over all the fabrics and chatting with him, but I liked to pat old Gracie. One day I saw the biggest horsefly on Gracie that could have ever existed without being a bee. I yanked out a piece of cloth and swatted that monster as hard as I could. Got it too. Gracie and Ma thought I had lost my wits, but Mr. Whitmarsh laughed and told me I had saved the day. If Gracie had been bitten, there's no telling what would have happened. Then he gave me the cloth and Ma was proud of my quick thinking. She made an apron out of that cloth and I always liked to see her use it. Gracie never thanked me, but I felt closer to her after that.

Yes, I remember the rag man who came around regularly, too. He was quiet and more businesslike, and his horse was a beauty. Ma used to save scraps of cloth to sell to him.

Then there was Maynard West, who used to deliver coal so that you could have the fun of that chore. Never saw him without a piece of chewing tobacco in his mouth. Once I saw him give a plug of that tobacco to his horse who chewed it thoughtfully and then swallowed it down. Lordy, I think even Gracie had more sense than that.

Seems like we got along just fine without malls and shopping centers back then. The traveling salesmen had everything we needed. What they didn't have we could find in the Marion groceries or the Sears Roebuck catalog. If those places didn't have it, then it wasn't a necessity. And that's what we grew up on. Use it up or wear it out, but make it last. That was Ma's way.

My pen is running out of ink, but remind me to tell you about another salesman we called Mr. Midnight. It's hard to find a pen that lasts these days.

Go out and shuffle along in some leaves. It will do you good.

As always,
Your brother,

d

Dear d,

We're in between seasons here in Maine. Fall has finished dropping her leaves all around us and winter is not yet ready to make her appearance, so here we sit in the doldrums of November. Can't do anything in my garden, but there is still some pruning to do and flower beds to be tucked in. But some days I'm more likely to stay put by the woodstove because my bones just don't want to carry me outside into the grey coldness.

When we were kids we didn't notice the weather so much. I remember each day being the same, but we weren't bored with it. There was always school and plenty of chores, but lots of free time too. Ma was pretty agreeable about letting us wander off as long as we were back for supper. And she didn't ask questions about where we had been, which was a saving grace for us all, but she wasn't so carefree about Grace.

Poor Grace had Ma's eye on her more than we ever did, and I was often glad I wasn't in her shoes. She had to help with Mrs. Taylor's washing while we were flying around on our fox-tailed bikes. Once in a while I find myself thinking about Grace and feel that life wasn't fair to her.

Remember how she loved dogs? She would pester Ma about having a dog more than any of us did, but still Ma wouldn't give in. Sometimes I think Ma was harder on Grace because she expected more out of her. Grace was the smart one, and pretty too, I guess, for a sister, and we all thought she would make something of herself. But she ran out of time. And that wasn't fair.

I read somewhere that the yo-yo didn't come to America until 1929. We were teenagers by then. How did we miss out on that? Guess that wasn't fair either.

Gerry wants me to fix the latch on the cellar door, so I'd better get to it. I like the time I spend writing to you, but sometimes when I finish, the remembering weighs too heavily on me, and I need to reacquaint myself with the world around me. It all comes down to realizing that we can't change what was any more than we can change what will be. So we'd better appreciate what is right now.

Love,

*C*liff and Gerry

Dear liff,

What do you mean we missed out on the age of the yo-yo? Maybe you were an old man by then, but I was still a whipper-snapper, and I remember having lots of fun with yo-yos. A simple toy but tricky to master. I was pretty good at it, but Monk Hall and Dingy Blankinship were the masters, and Squid Elsworth could handle two at a time.

I know what you mean about Ma being hard on Grace. But Grace didn't complain, except about the fact that all her friend's mothers let them have dogs. She sure did love animals, and more than once she came to my rescue over some critter I was trying to sneak into the house. Remember the frog hatching pail I kept in my closet?

I was determined to hatch my own frogs when I found that fascinating mass of jelly eggs in the cow pond at Grandpa's farm. I kept them in an old bucket outside in the sun behind the stone wall, but brought them inside on chilly days or rainy nights. Of course I never told Ma because I had a good idea how she would feel about it, and I had worked so hard at dragging that sloshing bucket all the way home with visions of pet frogs in my head. Grace found out in no time, and she was as excited as I was. Together we did a pretty good job of keeping our secret stash from Ma's quick eyes.

As spring turned into summer, our polliwogs still hadn't hatched but were looking awfully slimy, so we decided that they were getting too hot being outside in the sun, and that's how the bucket came to stay in my closet. Guess I forgot about it until I began noticing more mosquitoes than usual in my room, along with a distinctly unpleasant odor. So it didn't take Ma too long to track my hatching pail down. What a ruckus.

She was going on about a bucket of mosquito eggs in my closet and what was a mother to do and all that stuff, when Grace confessed that she had been in on the scheme and took half the blame. She didn't have to do that. I wouldn't have told, but Grace was unpredictable like that. Then she made matters worse by pointing out that if we had owned a dog we wouldn't have to have mosquitoes for pets. Sometimes she didn't know when enough was enough. Our Grace was first rate and I miss her still.

Cold in Marion these days, and the wind blows up the hill from the harbor bringing smells of seaweed. It's an old smell and sometimes a sad one, but that's just how it is.

As always,
Your brother,

Falmouth, Maine
November 28, 1995

Dear d,

We got about three inches of snow last night, and now it is pouring rain. Never can tell about the weather around here. I don't think I will go out today. It's one of those stay-by-the-wood-stove days.

I'd like to send Bob Taber a box of candy when I feel up to it. He sent me a package of cranberries from Marion, which I always look forward to. We grow a lot of things up here but haven't quite got the knack of growing cranberries. It's like getting a little bit of home when the cranberries come.

I have an old map that shows the brooks and streams around Marion that we used to know as kids. The one that comes through Sippican bog and Sparrow bog by Stano's Mill is called Burden's Brook. Bob Jenny's Brook is Aaron's Run on the old map of 1856.

We had sixteen of the family here on Thanksgiving. I realize how lucky I am to have my kids and grandkids around me. When I was a little fellow I used to envy the other kids when I saw them with their fathers. Maybe that's why I am so thankful for what I have now. But Uncle Amos and John Taber were sure good to us, weren't they? And there were many others who were kind to us and patient, too. John Swift, the blacksmith, was like that. Remember how we used to hang around his shop with the other men, and he always treated us equally? Always good for a tale or two. Some of the kids were afraid of how he looked, but that didn't matter to me. He was a good man.

I miss my plants at this time of year when spring seems so far away. And I miss the greenhouse from the estate here, where I worked for fifty years. Winter never seemed to find me when I was in the greenhouse, and I loved my work. I left Marion in

1934. I had a good time growing up there, but in my line of work there wasn't much to do. When I worked with George Malneck I knew shrubs and trees and flowers, but I needed greenhouse experience, so when the family moved to Maine, I came too, and here I have stayed for more than sixty years. It was a good move, and I have been happy here with Gerry and the family, but Marion has always stayed with me too.

Keep well and always carry a clean handkerchief in your pocket. Have fun at bingo, but don't spend too much. Hope you had a good Thanksgiving, too.

Love,

Cliff and Gerry

Dear liff,

Glad you had a good feast on Thanksgiving. It was quiet here, but some nice folks from the church invited me over and we had a good time. They have two dachshunds. Remember the dachshunds I used to have? Grace would have liked them for sure. The first dog was wonderful but the next was as troublesome as poison ivy.

I was so full of turkey and pie that I took a little nap when I got back, when all of a sudden that dingblasted fire siren went off. Deaf as I am, it nearly blasted me off of the couch, and this time it wasn't even me burning the bacon. Don't know why they can't have a normal siren. Doesn't seem like a hard problem to solve. One of these days I'll walk over to the fire station and straighten them out.

I haven't thought of John Swift for years, but when you wrote about him he was as clear as a summer day. We used to hang around his blacksmith shop as kids, and it seemed like a lot of men did. I don't think Ma knew how much we learned from those men or that she would approve, but we had a lot of free rein as boys, and I think she was glad of our acquaintances with the men of Marion. Or else she was just glad we weren't under foot. But I liked John Swift first rate. He was just easy to be with. Wasn't he a big fellow though? And he was always full of stories, some of which would match Mr. Midnight's tales, I think. He always had time to make us nail rings, too. We could watch him make them like magic, bending in the orange fire and turning into black metal out of the water.

Everyone liked John Swift but some were afraid of him because of that awful growth on the side of his face, and I don't mean only kids were afraid. I remember Uncle Amos fishing with him from the wharf across from his shop on the corner of Ryder's Lane. John took a drink of something in a mug and then handed it to Uncle Amos to share. But when he wasn't looking, Uncle Amos threw the mug in the water. I knew he was afraid he might catch whatever that growth was and wasn't taking any chances. I'm sure John must have felt this fear from folks, and, although he was a blustery man, it must have saddened him. Maybe that's why I did what I did. One day he offered me a nickel to touch that growth. A nickel in those days was like a gold piece to a kid, so I touched it and everyone laughed. But it was worth it, and I don't mean just for the money. I worried for a long time after that, but John Swift was my friend and I'm glad I did it.

There was another funny thing that John did. He had his gravestone engraved and ready to go. All it needed was the date filled in. It was set up in the cemetery too, just waiting for him. I came across it one day, and it said: "Nothing from nothing leaves nothing." An odd sort of epitaph I think, especially from someone who I remember as being full of laughter. But we never see all that is in a person, do we? Old John has been resting in peace beneath his gravestone for many a year now. I lost that nail ring long ago. Wish I still had it.

As always,
Your brother,

Dear d,

It is dark and cloudy here today and only about thirty-two degrees. Gerry and I went to church today, and the minister took in fifteen new members. Seems like we might be doing something right.

Gerry has been busy making wreaths with those great-smelling balsam boughs, and the whole house smells like Christmas. We put one on Judith's stone in the cemetery, and it looks very fitting. Folks up here say that you can tell the weather by looking at pine cones, but I'll be hornswaggled if I can tell. Supposedly the pieces of the cones open up if the weather will be fair and close up tight if a storm is coming. They always look the same to me, and I've been staring at pine cones all my life.

When we talked on Saturday, you got laughing about Mr. Midnight, some vendor from when we were kids. My memory is older than yours, so it's a bit dusty and I don't recall him. That wasn't his real name, was it?

Already the paper is full of Christmas advertising. I remember how Ma used to decorate for Christmas and how she was like a little girl again with all the surprises she planned. We always used to get our tree at Gram's. Remember how the best trees were around the fox holes in the back pasture? We used to see lots of foxes in Marion, especially around the marshes. Most folks would like to think that Sippican changed its name to Marion in honor of the person who was the Swamp Fox, but I think it was because of the real foxes that used to roam the swamps. Nowadays we buy our tree from the fire department in Cumberland. Not the same as cutting our own as kids, but these days we opt for convenience.

Christmas trees come in all sizes, but when a kid goes to pick one out only the tallest and widest will do. There was more than one Christmas when we brought home a tree about three feet taller than our living room ceiling. How we struggled to bring home the best tree, dragging it through the woods and across Converse Road, only to have Ma saw off the bottom. And how we protested! Then we made paper chains with lots of flour and water paste, and strung cranberries, and put on the few ornaments that Ma had saved over the years.

Reminds me of the glass pickle. Do you remember the one she liked so much? She had saved it from when she was a kid, and I think Grandpa had given it to her. There was some game she had played with it on Christmas morning, something about finding a hidden present, but I don't recall the particulars. Anyway, one Christmas I dropped it and it broke into a million purple slivers. I felt so bad because I knew it was special to her, even though I never could see the sense of a pickle at Christmas. But she didn't holler at me, just made me clean it up and then we went on to other things, but I saw her wipe away a tear. Seeing a tear from a mother's eye is just about the worst feeling for a boy at Christmas.

I never forgot about that old pickle ornament. Some years later I found another one in a shop so I bought it for her and she was very pleased. I knew it would never mean as much to her as that one from her father, but it made us both feel a little better. I wonder what ever became of that pickle?

Keep warm Ed, and do your walking inside these days. Those long halls at Marconi are perfect for that, and there's no truck traffic in them. Gerry needs me to help her with the wreaths now so I'll say good bye.

Love,

liff and Gerry

Dear liff,

Christmas is around the corner, as they say. I do remember those tree cutting expeditions we went on to Grandma's farm. Al always told us to think smaller, but we only thought with our eyes. Then Grace would laugh at us when we got home and pull out all the "I told you so" quotes she had been saving, mostly because she couldn't come with us in the first place. In those days there were strict limits for girl chores and boy chores.

Ma always managed to have Christmas surprises for us. Don't know how she did it on so little money and four kids to provide for, but she did. Of course she made lots of knitted things, which we were glad to have because, along with everything else, Marion was colder in those days, too. One thing Grace and I always asked her for though, which she never seemed to hear, was to have a dog. I asked at Christmas and on my birthday but she always said that she had enough to look after with the family. We would be hard pressed to find any faults with Ma, especially now when we look back on growing up, but if I had to pick out one I'd say it was her stubbornness about dogs.

Strange you don't remember Mr. Midnight. But since you are ever so much more ancient than I it is not surprising. Mr. Midnight's real name was Ralph Stuart, and he was a traveling salesman who came around to the ladies of Marion on a regular basis, like so many vendors in those times. He had a jalopy of a truck with canvas sides that rolled up to display his wares, and he looked mighty interesting to a boy like me because you could tell that he was a man of the world. Funny thing though, Ma would never let me come out when he drove up because she said he told naughty stories and said words that a boy shouldn't hear. I'd like to know what we hadn't heard by then. But Ma didn't realize that by keeping us away she made him all the more appealing, and soon Mr. Midnight had a reputation that was mysterious and romantic. Never knew why it was okay for her to hear those stories, being a lady and all, but she seemed to like Mr. Midnight just fine. She said she only talked with him because of the fine wares he peddled, but I think she found him mysterious too. All the other kids knew of him. They called him a true ladies' man, although I suspect the term was more innocent in those days. Although I never really talked with him at length, he stands out the most vividly in my mind among the traveling salesmen of Marion .

I do walk a lot in the halls here. Also I work out in the community room on the exercycle. The Christmas tree in there is nice. I don't have one in my apartment, so I like to look at it when I'm on the cycle. Of course, nothing on it is real like our trees from the farm, but I have all the memories tucked away and that will do. A person can live comfortably on memories. I do remember the purple glass pickle, but I don't remember you breaking it. Glad it wasn't me.

Some carollers from the church are coming over tonight. That will be nice. I never was much at singing but I do like to hear the old carols. Do you remember what a terrible singing voice Ma had? Didn't stop her from using it though, and somehow it was okay at Christmas. She sang louder than anyone I have ever known, but it's funny that I forget all the other singers and remember only her. A little like Mr. Midnight.

As always,
Your brother,

Falmouth, Maine
December 15, 1995

Dear d,

It is forty-four degrees and dark and rainy, so it's kind of dreary today. I just cut up a lot of cardboard boxes to take to the recycle center in Falmouth. As soon as I do, Gerry will be looking for boxes for Christmas presents and I will be in the soup. That's how it usually goes. I greased and tuned the snowblower this morning, so now I am ready for whatever winter wants to throw at me. I'll just throw it back.

The house is all decorated and sparkling and ready for the grandkids. Gerry does a nice job of turning this place into Santa's palace. Do you remember the paper bell Ma used to hang from the register over the stove? Don't know why that came to mind. It wasn't too colorful or shiny like the pickle and over the years it faded, but it was a traditional part of Christmas for us. I wonder whatever became of it. At least I didn't break it.

It was chilly in church yesterday. Guess we need some of those old-time sermons to heat things up. The old church in Yarmouth is on Brimstone Hill. Must have been named after all those fiery sermons preached up there. We heard some as kids. There was plenty of fire in the pulpits in Marion in those days.

You can't make JELL-O? How can anyone miss in making JELL-O? Guess you'd better read the directions the next time you make it. Ma would not be pleased with your cooking skills. You should also try instant oatmeal. It's real simple, and Gerry makes it for me with raisins in it. I bet even you could figure it out.

I would like to sit out in Bob Taber's shop and talk about the old-timers we used to know. Of course, no one called the other by his Christian name. It was normal to have nicknames back then, and some of them were doozers. Pete Hadley and Splint Winters came up with the most. The one that I liked best was "Cloggy Whistle Trigger" which he hung on Howard Blankinship. They used to call you "Quack" because of the way you walked. It's odd, but we didn't mind those names or feel insulted. It was just the thing to do and it was fun.

Time is wasting, and I have to get to those boxes. Stay warm, keep out of trouble, and try reading directions.

Love,

Cliff and Gerry

Marion, Mass.
December 21, 1995

Dear liff,

JELL-O is not the easiest thing to make.

I took the Council on Aging van into Fairhaven today to do some shopping. It's a good thing the town has that van or a lot of us old-timers would be starving. I can't see the shelves too well but the driver is very helpful and reads labels for me. You are lucky to have Gerry.

Some of those old nicknames were wonderful. Some that I remember with a chuckle were Ed Blankinship (Jigger), Manny Rose (Spider), Frank Costa (Rubber Jaws), Etta Hubbard (Squashneck), Norman Jenny (Bunky), Charlie Bowman (Oakum), Reuben Chase (Skinny), and Leslie Daggett (Tiny). There were others too, but I have forgotten their real names, like Stub Caswell, Bushelmouth Moore, Monk Hall, Tubby Dewhurst, Hocky Costa, Rammy Smith, and Sunny Morris. One of the best names was for Eddy Tripp. We called him Diddy because of the question, "Did he trip?" It was a lot of fun hanging a name on someone and having it stick.

I remember some of the old-time sermons you talked about. I don't remember so much what was said as much as how it was said. Mostly I was looking at the other kids squirming in their Sunday clothes, as I was.

Do you remember Mrs. Clark? She was what you'd call a pillar of the church, and she knew how important she was. Like everyone else in church, she had a pew that she always sat in. It's funny, but it still holds today. Everyone pretty much has a pew staked out. So you can imagine her astonishment when she came one Sunday to find a row of Tabor boys in HER pew.

Those were the days when Tabor students had to attend church, and I guess they miscalculated that day and took her space. She reacted like a bull finding the gate locked. You must have been in Maine by then, but I remember her standing in the aisle tapping her cane angrily. No one knew what to do. Finally an usher came down the aisle and pointed out that there were still plenty of pews available. That really got to her.

"Young man, I have always sat in this pew," she shouted, loud enough for everyone to hear. "My family paid for it in perpetuity, and I will not budge from this spot until these trespassers are evicted!"

Meekly, all the boys filed out to another pew.

Years later I saw her again walking down Cottage Street with her daughter. I asked how she was but she didn't answer.

"Mother," said her daughter. "He asked you how you were."

"I know," she snapped. "That's why I'm COGITATING!"

Hope you have a nice Christmas with all your family and grandkids. It's nice to have kids at Christmas, although yours are not so little anymore. I'm going to the parsonage for Christmas dinner, but I will call you. Maybe by then you'll have all the coal dust dumped out of your stocking! Merry Christmas to you both.

As always,
Your brother,

Falmouth, Maine
January 9, 1996

Dear Ed,

Clear and cold this morning, only fifteen degrees. When it warms up to twenty degrees, we will have to do some grocery shopping, as we always like to have a good supply on hand in the winter. Never can tell when we might have to hole up for a few days.

When Ma ran the house, she taught us that things were to be kept in good order, and we tried to do just that. One of my jobs was to keep coal and wood in the house and to clean out the ashes. I didn't especially like that job, but there were worse chores I could have had. Seems to me you never worked as hard as I did, but then I might be remembering with some envy since you were five years younger. All in all I think Al and I had the most to do. It never seemed like Grace had that much to do either, but then she was a girl and only had to do the household stuff. Nowadays it's different, but back then we had boy jobs and girl jobs. Ma had to do them both.

You could never say that Ma was lazy. She was always working. As if we weren't enough, she took in boarders too and saw to their needs and cooked for us all. Then she took in laundry for Hannah Taylor. I remember how hard she worked at that, and it was your job to deliver it. Not as bad a chore as shoveling ashes. Remember Henry Taber, who boarded with us until he got married? Then his brother Bill came to live with us. We were always close to the Tabers, especially after their dad died.

Where have all the Blankinships gone to? John had a boy, but he left the area, and I heard that he had a son who was a minister in Vermont.

Have you found anyone to play cribbage with yet? Nate Nye sure was good at it.

Been thinking about blueberries lately. I miss not having them around in the winter, but it was a small crop last summer. Too rainy, so we didn't have any left over to freeze. But the raspberries were good, and the grapes too, after the coons had taken their lot. Canned and frozen food from the store just isn't like from the garden. I miss that.

Looks like it's warming up a few degrees, so Gerry and I had better get to the grocery. Keep well and call some time.

Love,

*C*liff and Gerry

Marion, Mass.
January 23, 1996

Dear liff,

Cold here too, but not any snow. Got to get across Route 6 today to get a haircut. My white cane helps but I always add a prayer. My hair always did grow like the dickens and even though I am eighty-two years old it still grows faster than seaweed. When we were kids a haircut cost a dime. I sure wish that were true nowadays.

Speaking of hair, did I ever let you in on my haircutting scheme? If I didn't, it was because I didn't want Ma to find out and it was my own personal brainstorm. Ma always used to give me a dime to get my hair cut, and that must have been often because of the speed with which my hair grows.

I was supposed to get my hair cut by Jim Nelson, the barber who had his shop beneath the Cozy Theater. But between Clark Street and Main Street I came across a kindly farmer on Pleasant Street who offered to cut my hair for free. I liked that deal and was glad to take him up on the offer.

He plunked a bowl on my head and cut around it, and in no time it looked as if I had been to the barber's and back. I always remembered to thank him, but I never told him about the dime in my pocket. Of course, I took that dime right down to the store and traded it for candy. Ma never could figure out how I came back looking so pleased with a haircut that looked so bad.

Guess I was a rascal as a youngster, but you knew that. But I wasn't all that bad. Once in a while I'd share some of the candy with Grace. I felt sorry for her because she was a girl and couldn't get her hair cut as often as I did. She never asked how I came by such treats, but was glad at her good fortune. I had other tricks that I played on folks, and I guess I am old enough now to confess to them without fear of retribution. One of my favorites was the disappearing carrot trick.

I'd have to give Cousin Charlie some credit here because he was in cahoots with me. It was on Uncle Seth's farm where he had that big vegetable garden. Charlie and I would pull up the biggest, orangest carrots, brush off the dirt, and munch them right down to the tops. Then we would replant the tops in the dirt so no one, especially Uncle Seth, would suspect that the carrots were gone. But I bet Uncle Seth was annoyed at the moles and coons just like you. You see, I didn't learn all my bad habits from you. Carrots today don't taste as good as those earthy ones from our uncle's garden. Half of the goodness was in the fun.

Someday I'll find enough gumption to tell you about the watermelons we stole, but that's another story. Guess that's why Ma made sure we went to Sunday school each week in the Congregational Chapel. I still try to get to church each Sunday, and I sit in the farthest back pew by the pillar. Always have. And when I leave I shake hands with the pastor, and he says, "See you next week, Ed." Then I say, "Lord willing and if the devil don't want me." Makes him laugh, but if he only knew...

Keep dreaming of blueberries in January.

> As always,
> Your brother,
>
> d

Falmouth, Maine
January 26, 1996

Dear d,

Heavy white frost this morning, but cool and clear. My parsnips must be having a good rest under the ground with this weather.

Gerry and I were talking about some of the old-timers yesterday. I remember all the nicknames we gave each other. Funny to think about that now, but back then it was serious stuff. No one went by their God-given name, only their gang-given name. Then Gerry said something very true. "Cliff," she said, "We are the old-timers now." By golly, she was right. How did it happen so fast?

I have to get up enough steam to use the snowblower and clear the driveway and paths to the bird feeders. We have a big, hungry flock of mourning doves and lots of finches, along with cardinals and chickadees. I have used about five fifty-pound bags of sunflower seeds so far. Funny thing though, I don't mind feeding the birds because they are fun to watch, and I figure it is cheap entertainment. But I do mind feeding the chucks and coons in the summer because it's more like a battle with them.

I have a pan of tulips in bloom that I put up. There was a pan of jonquils, too, but they have all gone by. I like having flowers in the winter as much as having birds.

Do you remember fishing with Uncle Amos? Being five years younger than I, you probably remember different things, but Uncle Amos was especially good to us. There were a lot of men in the town who filled in for our dad, like Ike, who used to take us sailing just for fun. He'd let out those patched-up old sails and we'd fly over the water like winter birds. I miss that now that I'm landlocked, but I'll always remember the feeling. John Taber was good to us too. He used to take me with his own kids for hikes around the bogs and clamming at Aucoot. He was never too busy to include us. We learned a lot from those people, and I have tried to be like them over the years. I hope that someday I might be remembered like that.

Well, Quack, this old-timer had better get to the snow-blower. Don't forget to wear a hat when you go outside in this weather. Keeps the heat from leaving your head.

Love,

liff and Gerry

Cliff's bird feeder

Dear liff,

Gerry is right. We are the old-timers now. Don't know how it happened. Seems like yesterday we were Marion kids with unending days ahead of us, and now we are old-timers with precious few days left. If I could go back to being a boy in Marion, I would slow down and enjoy a day at a time. Wish we could tell today's kids that, but it's something they will have to figure out for themselves, probably when it's too late.

Lots of wood smoke in the air these days. I rather like it because it is an old smell that brings back memories of winter days when we were young. Ma didn't use much wood for burning because we had the coal stove, but the smell of wood was everywhere. Remember how Bob Taber and I used to cut wood to sell? We cut many a cord in our day and it was hard work. No chainsaws then. I remember one fiasco that folks today would call a rip-off.

Al Little, who was the postmaster then, told us about a woodlot that the Universalist Church owned, and he got us a job there. The deal was that we would cut the timber, clear the lot, and share the profits. At the time it was of no use to the church, and they paid only twenty-two cents an acre for taxes. Today a stamp costs more than that. So Bob and I set to work, and work it was. All in all we cut fifty-six cords of wood, which was no small task, but we were proud of the job and anticipated a tidy profit.

We arranged with Mr. Perry to sell him the whole kit and caboodle, but when the time came to make the deal he backed down. Tinker always said you could trust him about as far as you could throw a chimney by the smoke, and I guess he was right. So we were stuck with a ton of wood and the church had a nicely cleared lot, but neither of us had any money. We finally did sell that wood bit by bit, but it didn't turn out to be the fortune we thought it would be, and it took so long we were happy just to be rid of the last twig. Now when I go for my winter walks and smell the smoke in the air, I chuckle and think that someone may be burning the last of that wood we cut so long ago.

Stay inside these days and plan your spring garden. And when you sit by your woodstove, think of me.

As always,
Your brother,

Ed

Falmouth, Maine
February 6, 1996

Dear d,

We got more snow this past winter than I can ever remember. Close to thirty inches, the weatherman said. The mounds by the driveway are so high that it's hard to see around them, and pulling out into the street is tricky. It's funny to see car antennas with orange tennis balls on them going by the snow hills that line the roads. That's all we can see, tiny tennis balls going by. Glad I can stay home by the woodstove more often than not. It's a good companion.

I just finished my garden plan for this year. I always like to do that at this time of year. The pictures in the catalogues do my eyes and my spirit a world of good. I still have carrots, squash, and onions left, but due to dry weather this past summer I didn't get a good crop of spuds.

We have five bird feeders and three bags of suet around the house, so we have lots of birds, including cardinals and an assortment of unidentified flying feathered things. As always, the squirrels are pests, but they have to eat, too. I think they are related to chucks. They have the same sneaky ways about stealing food. Sometimes the coons come in the middle of the night and dump the feeders to get at the seeds. Maybe they're not hungry at all but like to make mischief just for a winter diversion. Learned it from the chucks, no doubt.

Do you remember that black girl in my class who played the violin so well? Her name was Eleanor, and I sometimes find myself wondering about her. I expected to find her in the Boston Symphony someday.

I was also thinking about our family today. I'm glad we three brothers got along so well together. Too many families don't these days, and you need to be able to count on families.

Like it or lump it, you've always got family to go through this life with, so it's better if you like them. Families are like woodstoves. Don't always need them as we branch out and make our own new families, but it's good to know that they are there and can be counted on in the cold times. Over the years, as the family dwindles, those of us left become more valuable. We shouldn't forget to be thankful for that.

I'm sending you a package of hankies today so that you can cry over your gambling losses!

Love,

liff and Gerry

Eleanor playing her violin at graduation

Marion, Mass.
February 23, 1996

Dear liff,

Guess the snow we were supposed to get got dumped on you. Keep that snowblower in good shape, but don't put those seed catalogs aside yet. When we were kids we had practically memorized the Sears Roebuck catalog. Ma couldn't afford much, but that didn't stop us from pestering her about things that we thought we absolutely had to have. Even so, she always came up with something special for Christmas or birthdays. I remember her reading it carefully, too, and I bet she was wishing for things she never got.

Mark Twain said that he grew up poor, but no one ever told him that, so he didn't know it. He had a fine time growing up and so did we. Ma gave us much more than we could have ordered from a catalog.

You asked if I remembered about Eleanor, the black girl in your class, and I do. I also know what became of her. Even though Eleanor was older we all knew her because I think she was the only black girl in the school. She was nice to us younger kids too. And Lordy, could she play the violin. Learned from her grandfather and played in the school orchestra.

Remember Mr. Oliveira, the music teacher? Every eighth-grade graduation he was to pick the most outstanding student in music to play for the commencement. That year there was no doubt that it had to be Eleanor. Now the way I heard it was that the Board of Education told Mr. Oliveira that it was unheard of for a black child to be given this honor. They wanted him to change his mind, but he stood firm. Eleanor played for your graduation and left everyone speechless. I even remember what she wore. It was the most beautiful long, white dress, and you could tell that she felt like a star.

In the fall we had a new music teacher. Mr. Oliveira had been asked to leave, which I think was a real shame. All he had done was pick the best student for the task and stick to his guns.

I never ran into Eleanor again, but I did bury her. Must have been thirty years later, I'd say. You know that I had a number of jobs in Marion and one of them was a grave digger. I remember a rainy April morning that was so cold I thought it should be snowing. I was standing by the stonewall in the Old Landing Cemetery trying not to look obvious, but I was anxious for the committal service to be over so I could finish my job and get on to other tasks. When everyone had left I prepared to lower the casket but was stopped by a shout. Two elderly black ladies had driven up and were hurrying over to me. They explained that they had driven some distance and were late, and asked if I might open the lid so that they could pay their respects.

Now I tell you, Cliff, I didn't get asked that often, and it wasn't my place to do such a thing, but the ladies were very convincing in the rain. So I opened the coffin. There she was, Eleanor, as pretty as I'd remembered and not more than forty-five, I'd say. I think she even wore the same white dress, at least it looked like it to me. The ladies thanked me and went on their way, but I closed the lid and stayed for a while. Didn't care about the rain anymore. I finished the job and I'm not ashamed to say that I cried for the loss of such a talent. It was as if no time had passed between that commencement day and the burying day, and Eleanor had somehow remained the same.

Now you went and made me cry all over again. Good thing I have your supply of new hankies.

As always,
Your brother,

Falmouth, Maine
March 3, 1996

Dear d,

I have put two washes through this morning and am going to take the trash to the recycle place when I go out to get the paper.

I was thinking about how it used to be when we first went to Silvershell Beach. There was only a dirt path to it, and I remember two bath houses that the Allens put up. There was a stone wharf there too, and Ike used to have his boats pulled out there. The brook at that time came down toward the McCormick place, but it was changed over to meet Sprague's Cove. We used to set up water wheels in that brook, remember? It was a lot of work but also a lot of fun.

I am shaky this morning since I forgot to take my shaky pills, so I hope you can make sense of this letter. The snow has begun to pull back and the deer are roaming again. I saw four in the yard by the hollow apple tree yesterday. I'm sure they are checking out the garden and memorizing it for summer. Can't wait to see the first signs of rhubarb and asparagus, but that's still a long way off. First come the snowdrops and crocuses. Gerry gets excited about the early flowers, but I like to think of rhubarb pudding. When the pussy willows come I sell them to the florist in town. She's real glad to get them and they look nice in arrangements of spring flowers, especially daffodils.

Remember all the pussy willows out in back of Grandpa's farm? We liked them mostly for pulling apart and firing at each other like furry snowballs. We had to work hard on his farm, even in the summer, but we managed to have our fun times too.

Even though it is already March, I started a fire in the woodstove this morning. It works real good in cold weather and keeps the oil furnace from running away with our wallets.

Had enough of the coal stove when I was a kid, and I calculate I shoveled enough coal to fill a whaler, so I've done my share. Wood is more pleasing. I like apple wood best when I can get it, but anything that burns is fine with me, except pine.

Better get to the recycle place. Your eyes will need a rest from trying to figure out this scribbling. Keep warm and watch out for little green men on St. Patrick's Day.

Love,

Cliff and Gerry

Marion, Mass.
March 9, 1996

Dear liff,

I don't know who would win if we had a contest for the shakiest writing. Gets so that I can't read my own writing, so it's a good thing Gerry is still young and spry.

I've been thinking about the islands lately. Maybe because these grey March days remind me of the isolation of the few who lived out there. Do you remember Little Island in the harbor? It was a pretty place and we could even swim to it. There was a little house on it and I recall an old man who lived there. I doubt if he owned it and was probably camping out there, but once in a while we'd see him row to shore to get supplies in town. He was a loner but he didn't mind our swimming around there. We didn't bother him and he didn't bother us, which was a good arrangement. Too bad all that came to an end in the hurricane of '38. The house and half the island disappeared, but that was long after the lone inhabitant had vacated or died.

Bird Island of course was much further out. We didn't get there too often but I remember the house and the big bell barn. I often thought it would be swell to live there. Billy Babcock did live there with his sister Helen. Did you know them? They came to school in the winter and boarded in town. I figured that the best part of living at Bird Island was waiting for Edward Rowe Snow, the flying Santa. Every Christmas he flew over lighthouses all around New England to drop sacks of goodies and sweets and surprises for the folks confined to the lighthouses out there. Billy said every time they heard a plane engine they'd run outside to see if it was Mr. Snow. One time they missed him because he came when they were still in Marion going to school, and this was a big disappointment. I wish Mr. Snow had dropped off things for us!

Helen used to tell of a lighthouse keeper from a century ago who had come out there with his wife to finish out a prison term. He was to work the lighthouse and live there but not allowed to leave. It was a prison without walls and, unfortunately, his wife was a prisoner too. But in those days a wife went wherever her husband did, no questions asked. The wife used to write to her sister that she feared for her life. Finally her sister and her sister's husband came out to the island to take her home with them, but she was nowhere to be found. The lighthouse keeper said that she had left already, but he wouldn't let them search the island and she was never seen again. Over the years rumor had it that she had been murdered and was buried in the cellar.

Helen used to say that on windy nights she could hear the poor lady crying for someone to free her from the island prison. I think Helen was trying to impress us and had a good imagination, but the other facts are true. Of course we'll never know now. Helen is still living but not in Marion. Sippican harbor will just have to keep that secret along with so many others.

Think I'll go look for pussy willows now. This has been a long letter and my legs need stretching. Enough of ghosts. I need to find spring.

As always,
Your brother,

Ed

Falmouth, Maine
March 13, 1996

Dear d,

I'm still painting trellises. It seems to be a never ending job but the clematis looks so pretty climbing all over them that I guess it's worth the work.

I'm having the house painted this spring as Gerry won't let me climb ladders anymore due to my advanced age. Such nonsense. I've always painted the house. I already have the shutters done and ready to be put up when those young painters finish.

I have put up my seed-starting gear in the cellar and I will probably sow pepper seed this week. I have my garden plan all made out and I sure hope I am up to doing it this year—that is, if Gerry and the chucks will let me.

Hardly seems like March already. I remember it was a balmy day in March when you almost got killed by Joe Treadway playing football. It was one of those rare days that teases you about spring but you know there's still plenty of winter left. Joe was a tough kid whose father had taught him to box but he had neglected to tell him how to be a good sport. We were all having a good time playing football behind the Tabor House because there were good fields there, and that was before the house was moved to make room for Sippican School. Joe got mad at you for some reason and tackled you with punches like a mad cow. We had to peel him off of you. By the time I got you home, you were a soggy mess of blood and tears.

Ma nearly hit the ceiling when we told her that Joe had picked on you unfairly. She stormed out of the house heading for Joe's place and she was gone for a long while. We were beginning to worry about Joe's well being. Ma was ordinarily an easy going kind of woman, and we were surprised how her sails could blow up so quickly. But when she came back she had the satisfied look of a fisherman with a good day's catch, well pleased with the job. Sure enough, Joe never did bother any of us again.

Guess I'd better get back to the trellises. I can almost hear the clematis pushing out buds and anxious to start the climb. Watch out for slippery spots when you are out walking.

Love,

Cliff and Gerry

Dear liff,

How did you remember about me and Joe Treadway? I hardly remember that myself, but I know that football has never been one of my favorite sports and maybe that's the reason why. We always enjoyed the fields behind the Tabor House and no one seemed to mind. But it sure was an amazing day when they moved that big old house. They went right through the woods with it down to Cottage Street. With horses, no less! Couldn't do that today, although I've seen plenty of houses split apart and moved in Marion with the help of fancy machinery. I think the whole town was there to watch. It was like watching the high wire act in the circus, exciting and daring at the same time. Never saw the likes of such commotion. Some were taking bets about the likelihood of its slipping off the rollers and smashing into the swamp, and I think some were disappointed when that didn't happen. All in all it was a sight to see.

Then they took down our school where Bicentennial Park is now and built a smart looking new one across the street. I always thought that was too bad. It was a good school, and all our memories were torn down with it. I suppose that is progress, but sometimes it hurts.

I wonder what Elizabeth Taber thought of all that progress. Did you know she used to smoke cigars?

Anyway, I think Gerry is right. You shouldn't be on ladders or under them, either. Maybe it's time to cut back on all the work you do around that place, especially in the garden. You know what they say about taking time to smell the roses. Not a bad idea.

Did you know that one cow can produce up to a hundred pounds of manure in a day? I heard that on the radio, and it's hard to believe unless you're hurrying home across Grandpa's farm fields. The Dexters settled that farm back in 1702, so there were lots of years to build up manure. Seems like our ancestors have been around here for centuries and that's a good feeling. The fields that used to be full of manure are now full of houses, and not much of the old farm remains except for the memories in our heads, just like the school. When we're gone they will be gone, too. Maybe that's why I've kept your letters all these years. Hope you've kept mine too. Some day they might be important to our kids.

Keep off those ladders and I'll give up football.

As always,
Your brother,

Ed

Falmouth, Maine
April 6, 1996

Dear Ed,

Clear and cold here this morning. When we got up it was blowing like a gale outside. Maybe we slept through spring and it's really November now. This time of year always makes me think of Ma and how she couldn't wait to pick the little flowers and put them in cups around the house. They didn't last long

Ma's cup of flowers

but it was a pretty sight. She would have bunches of mayflowers and violets in our every day cups looking delicate and colorful on the window sills.

Lots of new development around Falmouth these days. Seems a shame to see all the trees go down for new houses, but I hear that Marion is having the same growth. Still no call to cut down the old trees, especially the flowering ones like the apples. When we were young the town was full of great elm trees and wooded areas and fields nearby. Not so anymore. And why did the people who bought our house go and cut down the golden chain tree you planted for Nellie? I don't understand the thinking behind the chain saw, and it makes me more sad than mad. John Blankinship once told me that "They have stopped making land, but they are still making people." Trouble is, it doesn't take as long to build a person as it does to grow a beautiful tree.

I wonder why there are no more Blankinships in Marion when there used to be so many? Do you remember Joe Blankinship and his squeezebox? All the kids loved to hear him squeeze a mighty sound out of that little thing, and it would set our toes a-tapping.

Things do change, don't they? No one plays or hears a squeezebox any more, and this cold will turn into spring sooner or later. Take it easy, Ed, and keep a lookout for snowdrops.

Love,

*C*liff and Gerry

Marion, Mass.
April 14, 1996

Dear liff,

Everyone has a different opinion about things changing. I've heard that the more things change the more they stay the same. Forget who said that but it's true.

You should see our old house now. Painted in a rosy color with dark trim and it looks very nice, but nothing like it did when we were kids seventy years ago. Still, it will always be our house. Whenever I go by, I'm glad they fixed it up but it makes me a little sad, too. They never should have cut that golden chain tree down. I planted it on Mother's Day for my Nellie and we watched it grow over the years. Nellie used to say the tree was full of waving, welcoming yellow coils, and then she'd laugh because spring always made her happy, like Ma. I loved it when Nellie laughed. It still hurts to think about her. I expect you feel that way about your Judith. She was such a pretty little thing and you had her for so short a time. Seems like we didn't have our sister Grace for very long either. Time is a funny thing.

Sometimes I hear Ma calling me from upstairs just as she did when she discovered the frog hatching pail in my closet. Then some days I can't remember how she looked. And sometimes when I wake up I can smell balsam and I think it's Christmas morning and I'm late.

Everyone is already downstairs, you and Al and Grace, and Ma is hanging her glass pickle. Then before I can join you it's all gone, but the memory is so real it's hard to believe that it wasn't happening.

And on some foggy days, when the window is open and the winds are blowing off shore, I can smell the salt from the water and suddenly I'm back in the old boat with bushels of quahogs at my feet. Some nights when I look at the moon I can still believe it is as big as Ma's washtub.

Remember the old whalers who used to sit on Blankinship's store steps and tell about their adventures at sea? I think we've traded places. We're the old codgers now living on memories. There are days when I'm more alive in those memories than I am in these last years of the twentieth century, and the confusion leaves a sadness in me that's hard to put aside. That's when I'm glad to have you, Cliff, and to have Marion. Because the more Marion changes, the more it stays the same. We were lucky to grow up here.

Think I'll go out for a walk and pick some flowers for my cup.

As always,
Your brother,

Afterword

Ed filled many cups with flowers in his final years in Marion. The familiar sight of the tall man with the thick white hair trudging along the sidewalks ended when he moved from the house on Clark Street where he was born to Marconi Village eighty-three years later. Ed continued to walk daily, although

Ed and Cliff Ashley

busy Route 6 cut him off from the village, and failing health limited the distance he could cover. Sometimes he would rake the pine needles at the VFW or explore the paths behind the Marconi tower, but eventually even that became too difficult. With poor eyesight further limiting his excursions, he spent most of his days in a be-draggled, under-stuffed chair reminiscing about his boyhood adventures in Marion, Massachusetts.

When Cliff died in 1998, Ed lost not only a brother but also his best friend, and the spark of joy that always crinkled his eyes was forever gone. Ed died quietly a few months later and was buried beside his beloved Nellie in Evergreen Cemetery. He had finally reached the "washtub moon." A short distance away, his house still stands as a last silent witness to the memory of a family that lived and loved and flourished in the gentle times and friendly streets of Marion.

About the Editor

Diane deManbey Duebber

The Ed Letters: Memories of a New England Boyhood is Diane deManbey Duebber's third published book. She developed the concept for it while employed by the Marion, Massachusetts Council on Aging, where part of her job was to read mail to the elderly Ed Ashley. Recognizing the historical value of the nostalgic letters Ed's brother, Cliff, wrote to him every week, she set out to put Ed's memories into writing as well. She chose to record them in the form of reply letters, pairing them with the best of Cliff's correspondence to create this unique and revealing collection of memories and stories from a bygone era.

Ms. Duebber's other books are *The Strange Case of the Pettis Murders* and *The Great East Thompson Train Crash*. She lives with her husband and daughter in Thompson, Connecticut and is a teacher at the Rectory School in nearby Pomfret. In addition to writing about historical subjects, she enjoys children's literature, antiques, and folk singing.